Bible
Politics

Jesus words appear in Red Text

To St. Jane House,

Thank you for your great work !

Bible
Politics

Over 200 Bible Scripture Examples

STEVE D. BRACHT

BIBLE POLITICS

By Steve D. Bracht

Scripture quotations taken from the *New American Standard Bible®*, Copyright © 1960, 1962, 1963, 1968, 1971, 1972, 1973, 1975, 1977, 1995 by The Lockman Foundation. Used by permission. (www.Lockman.org)

Scripture quotations taken from the *Amplified® Bible*, Copyright © 1954, 1958, 1962, 1964, 1965, 1987 by The Lockman Foundation. Used by permission. (www.Lockman.org)

Scripture is taken from *GOD'S WORD®*, © 1995 God's Word to the Nations. Used by permission of Baker Publishing Group.

"Scripture taken from *The Message.* Copyright © 1993, 1994, 1995, 1996, 2000, 2001, 2002. Used by permission of NavPress Publishing Group.

"Scripture taken from the *New King James Version®*. Copyright © 1982 by Thomas Nelson, Inc. Used by permission. All rights reserved.

The Voice: Scripture taken from The Voice™. Copyright © 2008 by Ecclesia Bible Society. Used by permission. All rights reserved.

King James Version (KJV) Public Domain

Published by iLoveTruth Publishing

TABLE OF CONTENTS

ABOUT THE AUTHOR

I, Steve Bracht am a very simple, very average ordinary man, and if it were not for this scripture in 1ˢᵗ Corinthians chapter 1, I probably wouldn't have compiled these scriptures to put this book together in the first place, and just for the record, I am not trying to shame anyone.

1 Corinthians 1:26-31 (NASB)
[26] For consider your calling, brethren, that there were not many wise according to the flesh, not many mighty, not many noble; [27] but God has chosen the foolish things of the world to shame the wise, and God has chosen the weak things of the world to shame the things which are strong, [28] and the base things of the world and the despised God has chosen, the things that are not, so that He may nullify the things that are, [29] so that no man may boast before God. [30] But by His doing you are in Christ Jesus, who became to us wisdom from God, and righteousness and sanctification, and redemption, [31] so that, just as it is written, "LET HIM WHO BOASTS, BOAST IN THE LORD."

But I do read my bible, and I do understand, and know God, well enough, to have been passionate to persevere in getting this message of His word out to the public.

Jeremiah 9:23-24 (NASB)

[23] Thus says the Lord, "Let not a wise man boast of his wisdom, and let not the mighty man boast of his might, let not a rich man boast of his riches; [24] but let him who boasts boast of this, that he understands and knows Me, that I am the Lord who exercises lovingkindness, justice and righteousness on earth; for I delight in these things," declares the Lord.

So I know that God's children who hold a political office will also delight in exercising lovingkindness, justice, and righteousness onto all people, just as their heavenly father does.

INTRODUCTION
God Loves and Cares About the Poor, Needy, Hungry, Helpless, Orphan, Afflicted, Widow, Fatherless, Alien (Immigrant), Stranger and All Who are Oppressed by the Oppressors.

⌇

So why bring up a subject like bible politics you ask, especially with the separation of church and state in America? Simply because there are many politicians who want us to know they are Christian, in their attempt to win over the Christian voters, yet far too often these "Christian" politicians do not represent true biblical Christianity, as they attempt to cut huge dollar amounts from good government services that help the vast majority of Americans including all of the less fortunate.

These so called "Christian" politicians are continually creating many more needy people as they take from the majority and the poor, only to give every cut back to the wealthiest Americans in ever increasing tax breaks. This is absolutely not true Christianity in action, but more realistically reverse Christianity. One of the most disturbing things to me is that these people are elected saying things like "morals" and "family values."

So this book comes to you as a direct result of the Christian name being used by politicians, then being completely misrepresented by them in their law making. The bible scriptures in this book prove that God is all for a good government that helps all of its people with basic needs at the very least, because true biblical Christianity eliminates the needs of those in need. Therefore, we will start with a very simple, yet very solid foundational teaching from Jesus Christ Himself that clearly separates good politics from bad politics. Then we will look at a brief side by side comparison of the Democrat and Republicans way of governing the people's money, which are very opposite of one another. We will then proceed with the many other politically relatable bible scriptures, and lastly, we will look at the two subjects that Jesus never talked about, abortions and gays, which for the most part have taken the American churches eyes and hearts off of those who ARE very near and dear to the heart of God, the poor, needy, hungry, helpless, orphan, afflicted, widow, fatherless, alien (immigrant), stranger and all who are oppressed.

I conclude this introduction by asking you to please read these bible scriptures with an open heart, slowly, because I believe they speak very loudly and clearly for themselves, and for that reason, I have consistently tried to keep my own comments to a minimum. I thank you very much for being interested in this subject and for your support of the needy worldwide.

CHAPTER ONE
Jesus
7 Examples of Why His Words Are Important
Jesus Words Should be of Highest Value if You're a Christian

Nearly all of my Christian friends who I've met in church groups usually want to talk about the U.S. constitution whenever politics are brought up. They talk against a government that helps people with such things as healthcare and social security, then they will say that God never intended for government to do such things as these for the people. I strongly disagree with them only because their bible that they carry to church also strongly disagrees with them on these and other issues of government. This book is about bible politics, so we will not be looking at the U.S. constitution, but instead we will look at what is important to God, and we will see how our political opinions line up to His will, by using His words. And we will start with Jesus explaining why hearing and doing His words are so important. As we go through this book I will only try to back up what the scriptures say with what seems to be the very obvious political choices that we should be making as Christians.

Luke 6:46-49 (NASB)
Builders and Foundations

46 Why do you call Me, 'Lord, Lord,' and do not do what I say? 47 Everyone who comes to Me and hears My words and acts on them, I will show you whom he is like: 48 he is like a man building a house, who

dug deep and laid a foundation on the rock; and when a flood occurred, the torrent burst against that house and could not shake it, because it had been well built. [49] But the one who has heard and has not acted accordingly, is like a man who built a house on the ground without any foundation; and the torrent burst against it and immediately it collapsed, and the ruin of that house was great.

John 8:31-32 (NASB)
The Truth Will Make You Free
[31] So Jesus was saying to those Jews who had believed Him, "If you continue in My word, then you are truly disciples of Mine; [32] and you will know the truth, and the truth will make you free."

Luke 8:19-21 (NASB)
[19] And His mother and brothers came to Him, and they were unable to get to Him because of the crowd. [20] And it was reported to Him, "Your mother and Your brothers are standing outside, wishing to see You." [21] But He answered and said to them, "My mother and My brothers are these who hear the word of God and do it."

Luke 11:27-28 (NASB)
[27] While Jesus was saying these things, one of the women in the crowd raised her voice and said to Him, "Blessed is the womb that bore You and the breasts at which You nursed." [28] But He said, "On the contrary, blessed are those who hear the word of God and observe it."

John 7:14-18 (NASB)

[14] But when it was now the midst of the feast Jesus went up into the temple, and began to teach. [15] The Jews then were astonished, saying, "How has this man become learned, having never been educated?" [16] So Jesus answered them and said, "My teaching is not Mine, but His who sent Me. [17] If anyone is willing to do His will, he will know of the teaching, whether it is of God or whether I speak from Myself. [18] He who speaks from himself seeks his own glory; but He who is seeking the glory of the One who sent Him, He is true, and there is no unrighteousness in Him."

John 14:23-24 (NASB)

[23] Jesus answered and said to him,"If anyone loves Me, he will keep My word; and My Father will love him, and We will come to him and make Our abode with him. [24] He who does not love Me does not keep My words; and the word which you hear is not Mine, but the Father's who sent Me.

John 12:47-48 (NASB)

[47] If anyone hears My sayings and does not keep them, I do not judge him; for I did not come to judge the world, but to save the world. [48] He who rejects Me and does not receive My sayings, has one who judges him; the word I spoke is what will judge him at the last day.

CHAPTER TWO
Laying a Solid Foundation Using Jesus Christ's Words to Test the Christianity of Our Political Decisions

∽

Matthew 22:34-40 (NASB)

[34] But when the Pharisees heard that Jesus had silenced the Sadducees, they gathered themselves together. [35] One of them, a lawyer, asked Him a question, testing Him, [36] "Teacher, which is the great commandment in the Law?" [37] And He said to him, "'YOU SHALL LOVE THE LORD YOUR GOD WITH ALL YOUR HEART, AND WITH ALL YOUR SOUL, AND WITH ALL YOUR MIND.' [38] This is the great and foremost commandment. [39] The second is like it, 'YOU SHALL LOVE YOUR NEIGHBOR AS YOURSELF.' [40] On these two commandments depend the whole Law and the Prophets."

I mourn when I consider the condition of our world's people today as a whole. I mourn for all of the suffering, as there is so much needless suffering, these things should not be. Why have we let things get so out of control? I wonder how much more righteous our world could be if people and governments would always keep conscious of, and live by Jesus words here from Matthew Chapter 22. Just think how this would change what is wrong, as long as we were thinking honestly about it, towards one another. Individuals and leaders together, and leaders of the nations together. Then we would be so much more like the Kingdom of God here on Earth. How wonderful this world would be. No more hungry or homeless people, no more unhealthy people who can't afford their medications, no more premature deaths because people can't afford the medical needs they require. No more people living in filthy rotten destitute places that are completely unsanitary, full of disease, with no sanitary sewer systems or running water, full of precious people who don't know where their next meal is coming from, or when it will be. No more helpless or hopeless people anywhere, it surely could be done. If our nations worked collectively together to eliminate world hunger and poverty. This and so many other good things could be done if our nations didn't spend so much on war, especially America. Which world leaders do you believe are closer to doing Jesus will, the leaders who want to spend less on war so all of the people could have free healthcare, or the leaders that would rather the people suffer while all the massive war spending continues? Which would you say are loving their neighbor as themselves?

Love Your Neighbor as Yourself.

Notice how Jesus said "on these two commandments depend the whole law and the prophets." Jesus has undeniably explained the importance of loving your neighbor as yourself, as being so important, that it's in the greatest commandment of all. To me, whether I am a Christian politician, or a Christian voter, I need to run every political issue through this scripture, to see which side of the issue at hand I should be supporting. Also notice Jesus said "the second is like it", in other words, loving your neighbor as yourself is actually like loving God with all your heart, with all your soul, and with all your mind. I strongly believe this is a higher order of love, than just loving someone. If I have to love others as myself, I truthfully can't say that I have, until I have tried with all my mind to put myself in that persons shoes, but then I have only thought about them rightfully, they still have a need until I help to meet that need, if I am able. I believe that until we are willing as a nation, and as individuals to at least try to put ourselves in the shoes of those who are suffering or could potentially suffer, we will never be able to understand, or do, what loving our neighbor as ourself truly means. It is impossible for us to love our neighbor as ourself, if we are not willing to put ourselves in their shoes, this requires mercy, thinking and action, to do what is most right for them. Most of the time it's also going to cost money to love God, by loving His people, instead of loving money, more than people, which brings us to our next scripture of great foundational importance.

> ### Matthew 6:24 (NASB)
> [24] "No one can serve two masters; for either he will hate the one and love the other, or he will be devoted to one and despise the other. You cannot serve God and wealth."

Now that we have established the fact that loving our neighbor as ourself is a major part of loving God, it is very evident how to break this scripture from Matthew 6:24 down politically. I believe this is perhaps the most politically relatable scripture in the bible. What could possibly get in the way of the Lord's delight of exercising lovingkindness, justice and righteousness for all on earth through His servants? Money of course! Self-interest! Nearly every time a politician votes on a bill if not every time, he or she speaks of which Master he has chosen to serve that day. Either God, by voting for the betterment of the people, or money, when the politician votes against the people's best interest, to serve his own financial gain, from the corporations' lobbyists, whose interest are so often against the vast majority of the people, and they pay him to vote against the people, for their own gain. It's a constant battle in Washington that the people seem to lose now more than ever. If you are a politician who claims to be Christian, you should always be on the side of the people, because true Christianity, eliminates need as you will see, and God loves and cares about the poor, needy, hungry, helpless, orphan, afflicted, widow, fatherless, alien (immigrant) stranger, and all who are oppressed by the oppressors. The oppressors are living well now, but biblically I surely don't envy their future. The vast majority of scriptures in this book completely support a government that cares about the large group of people just mentioned. I separated these two scripture examples as very foundational political examples because they clearly separate good politics from bad, by asking us to question which side is loving people the most, and loving money the least. I believe these two would be all you would need to make right political decisions for a nation, and I encourage you to use them for every political issue. I also encourage you to read your whole bible all the more.

If a politician is practicing true biblical Christianity, he will be truly concerned about eliminating need from the people, and will be supportive of solutions that eliminate need while looking out for the people's best interest. This politician will not participate in oppressing the people but will remember that true Christianity eliminates need and loves and cares for the poor, needy, hungry, helpless, orphan, afflicted, widow, fatherless, alien (immigrant) stranger, and all who are oppressed by the oppressors. It is our job as voters to identify which of our political parties are doing the oppressing, and do our best to vote them out of office for our lifetime. Just as a tree is known by its fruit, Jesus said so are we. It is not calling ourselves Christian that makes us Christian, its believing what our bibles say and doing our best to live it out. Our Christianity should be observed by our love for people, whatever the cost.

Matthew 7:15-29 (NASB)
A Tree and Its Fruit

[15] "Beware of the false prophets, who come to you in sheep's clothing, but inwardly are ravenous wolves. [16] You will know them by their fruits. Grapes are not gathered from thorn bushes nor figs from thistles, are they? [17] So every good tree bears good fruit, but the bad tree bears bad fruit. [18] A good tree cannot produce bad fruit, nor can a bad tree

produce good fruit. [19] Every tree that does not bear good fruit is cut down and thrown into the fire. [20] So then, you will know them by their fruits.

[21] "Not everyone who says to Me, 'Lord, Lord, will enter the kingdom of heaven, but he who does the will of My Father who is in heaven will enter. [22] Many will say to Me on that day, 'Lord, Lord, did we not prophesy in Your name, and in Your name cast out demons, and in Your name perform many miracles?' [23] And then I will declare to them, 'I never knew you; DEPART FROM ME, YOU WHO PRACTICE LAWLESSNESS.'

The Two Foundations

[24] "Therefore everyone who hears these words of Mine and acts on them, may be compared to a wise man who built his house on the rock. [25] And the rain fell, and the floods came, and the winds blew and slammed against that house; and yet it did not fall, for it had been founded on the rock. [26] Everyone who hears these words of Mine and does not act on them, will be like a foolish man who built his house on the sand. [27] The rain fell, and the floods came, and the winds blew and slammed against that house; and it fell – and great was its fall."

[28] When Jesus had finished these words, the crowds were amazed at His teaching; [29] for He was teaching them as one having authority, and not as their scribes.

CHAPTER THREE
A Brief Overview of America's Two Major Political Parties
Side by Side

∽

The More Liberal Democrats

And

The Conservative Republicans

The (More Liberal) Democrat Way of Governing the People's Money.

Tax the wealthiest 1% of Americans adequately enough

AND

Spend less on defense for war

In order for America to provide its people:

• Very affordable healthcare for all people, keep Medicare and Medicaid strong.

• Keep Social Security strong, keep retirement age 62.

• Well-funded quality public schools, quality teachers, books, sports

• Well-funded city bus lines, subways, inexpensive public transportation for all.

• Well-funded city parks and public libraries.

• Well-funded street, highway, and bridge repair to keep roads smooth and safe.

• Well-funded public utility works, lights, water, sewer, snow removal, grass cutting, etc.

• Well-funded police and fire protection for all.

• Well-funded continued research in alternative clean energy sources such as solar, wind & others such as electric vehicles to create jobs and become less reliant on fossil fuels.

• Well-funded E.P.A. Environmental Protection Agency to help ensure clean air and water for all through government regulation of corporate polluters, to keep them honest and to keep pollution to the lowest levels possible.

• Well-funded food inspection.

• Well-funded assistance for food stamps and heat assistance for the poor, many who work.

The Conservative Republican Way of Governing the People's Money.

Reduce taxes on the wealthiest 1% as much as possible

AND

Spend more on defense for war

By cutting funding to government services for the people such as:

• Cut Medicare and Medicaid

• Cut Social Security and raise the retirement age

• Cut public education, schools, teachers, books, sports

• Cut funding to bus lines and affordable public transportation

• Cut funding to city parks and public libraries

• Cut street, highway and bridge repair

• Cut public utility works

• Cut police officers and firefighters

• Cut research in alternative clean energy sources such as solar, wind, and electric vehicles

• Cut E.P.A. Environmental Protection Agency and deregulate corporations to freely pollute the air and water keeping pollution on the rise, making some water undrinkable and air dangerous to breath.

• Cut food inspection

• Cut assistance for food stamps and heat assistance for the poor, many of whom work.

Other Differences about Democrats

(No corporate (for profit) control of government)

• Keep police and firefighters government controlled and not owned and operated by for profit corporations.

• Keep prisons government operated and not owned and operated by for profit corporations.

• Keep our 238 year old postal system government operated and not owned and operated by for profit corporations because it's never taken any tax dollars to operate.

• Keep government regulation of banks for the protection of the people to keep banks accountable and honest, also keeping the FDIC to ensure most peoples' savings in banks are safe.

• Keep sex education and abstinence training and regulate insurers to provide contraception to attempt to keep abortions and unwanted pregnancies to a minimum.

• Let immigrants become citizens, work, and pay tax to help the economy.

• Keep unions strong to give working people the strong voice of collective bargaining against corporate greed.

• In favor of the National Labor Relations Board for the American worker to have rights.

• Keep jobs in America instead of shipping them overseas.

• Strengthen the Voting Rights Act of 1965 to keep voting rights for all people fair, easy and strong. No difficult forms of ID required. Keep accessible same day registration. Make voting faster and easier to keep length of voting lines as short as possible.

• Democrats are very much against the sequester cuts which are not necessary and do nothing but hurt many people along with hurting America's economy.

Other Differences About Republicans

(Allow private corporations to take control of government services for profit)

• Allow private corporations to own and operate police officers and firefighters for profit.

• Allow private (for profit) corporations to own and operate prisons instead of government.

• Allow private corporations to take over America's successful 238 year old postal system for profit.

• Deregulate banks and enable them to be much less accountable for their actions.

• Cut sex education and contraception coverage.

• Spend billions of dollars keeping immigrants illegal and unable to pay tax into our government.

• Get rid of unions and the working people's voice to collectively bargain against corporate greed.

• Not in favor of the National Labor Relations Board for the American worker to have rights.

• In favor of shipping American jobs overseas.

• Weaken the Voting Rights Act of 1965 to make voting more difficult. Harder and more expensive forms of I.D. required. Some ending of accessible same day registration. Longer voting lines are inevitable with the Republican voter ID laws.

• Republicans are in favor of the sequester cuts.

CHAPTER FOUR
More of Jesus Words From the Gospels
Of Matthew Mark Luke & John

∾

Matthew 25:31-46 (NASB)
The Judgment

[31]"But when the Son of Man comes in His glory, and all the angels with Him, then He will sit on His glorious throne. [32]All the nations will be gathered before Him; and He will separate them from one another, as the shepherd separates the sheep from the goats; [33]and He will put the sheep on His right, and the goats on the left. [34]"Then the King will say to those on His right, 'Come, you who are blessed of My Father, inherit the kingdom prepared for you from the foundation of the world. [35] For I was hungry, and you gave Me something to eat; I was thirsty, and you gave Me something to drink; I was a stranger, and you invited Me in; [36] naked, and you clothed Me; I was sick, and you visited Me; I was in prison, and you came to Me.' [37] Then the righteous will answer Him, 'Lord, when did we see You hungry, and feed You, or thirsty, and give You something to drink? [38] And when did we see You a stranger, and invite You in, or naked, and clothe You? [39] When did we see You sick, or in prison, and come to You?' [40] The King will answer

and say to them, 'Truly I say to you, to the extent that you did it to one of these brothers of Mine, even the least of them, you did it to Me.'
[41] "Then He will also say to those on His left, 'Depart from Me, accursed ones, into the eternal fire which has been prepared for the devil and his angels; [42] for I was hungry, and you gave Me nothing to eat; I was thirsty, and you gave Me nothing to drink; [43] I was a stranger, and you did not invite Me in; naked, and you did not clothe Me; sick, and in prison, and you did not visit Me.' [44] Then they themselves also will answer, 'Lord, when did we see You hungry, or thirsty, or a stranger, or naked, or sick, or in prison, and did not take care of You?' [45] Then He will answer them, 'Truly I say to you, to the extent that you did not do it to one of the least of these, you did not do it to Me.' [46] These will go away into eternal punishment, but the righteous into eternal life."

Where Will You Stand?

Whether you believe in God or not, if the bible is true, there is an extremely high chance, that you will be there, where Jesus is describing someday, like it or not.

The big question is, which side of Jesus would your current actions predestine you to be on, His right, or left? Where will you be? Are you good to people that have needs or are you coldhearted? Are you loving people or money? Are you a Christian that's been fighting vehemently against affordable healthcare for all? Which sides actions does your life mimic? Which side's actions does your political party of choice mimic? Does Jesus say "I was rich, and needed another tax break? Does He show concern for the wealthy here? He does not. He is concerned about everyone though, especially the least of these, the poorest, sickest and most helpless among us. Also notice He is speaking to the nations. Yes, Jesus cares very much about how our governments treat the people.

Mark 3:1-6 (NASB)

Jesus Heals on the Sabbath

[1] He entered again into a synagogue; and a man was there whose hand was withered. [2] They were watching Him **to see** if He would heal him on the Sabbath, so that they might accuse Him. [3] He said to the man with the withered hand, "Get up and come forward!" [4] And He said to them, "Is it lawful to do good or to do harm on the Sabbath, to save a life or to kill?" But they kept silent. [5] After looking around at them with anger, grieved at their hardness of heart, He said to the man, "Stretch out your hand." And he stretched it out, and his hand was restored. [6] The Pharisees went out and immediately began conspiring with the Herodians against Him, as to how they might destroy Him.

Is it lawful to do good or to do harm, to SAVE a life or to kill? If it was JESUS will to heal this man on the Sabbath day (the day of rest and religious observance among Jews) then it is absolutely true for it to be His will to save life every day. Are you a Christian that is against affordable healthcare for all, and also against Jesus will in this scripture?

Luke 10:25-37 (NASB)

[25] And a lawyer stood up and put Him to the test, saying, "Teacher, what shall I do to inherit eternal life?" [26] And He said to him, "What is written in the Law? How does it read to you?" [27] And he answered, "YOU SHALL LOVE THE LORD YOUR GOD WITH ALL YOUR HEART, AND WITH ALL YOUR SOUL, AND WITH ALL

YOUR STRENGTH, AND WITH ALL YOUR MIND; AND YOUR NEIGHBOR AS YOURSELF." [28] And He said to him, "You have answered correctly; DO THIS AND YOU WILL LIVE." [29] But wishing to justify *himself, he said to Jesus, "And who is my neighbor?"*

The Good Samaritan

Jesus replied and said, [30]"A man was going down from Jerusalem to Jericho, and fell among robbers, and they stripped him and beat him, and went away leaving him half dead. [31]And by chance a priest was going down on that road, and when he saw him, he passed by on the other side. [32] Likewise a Levite also, when he came to the place and saw him, passed by on the other side. [33] But a Samaritan, who was on a journey, came upon him; and when he saw him, he felt compassion, [34] and came to him and bandaged up his wounds, pouring oil and wine on them; and he put him on his own beast, and brought him to an inn and took care of him. [35] On the next day he took out two denarii and gave them to the innkeeper and said, 'Take care of him; and whatever more you spend, when I return I will repay you.' [36] Which of these three do you think proved to be a neighbor to the man who fell into the robbers' hands?" [37] And he said, "The one who showed mercy toward him." Then Jesus said to him, "Go and do the same."

Jesus said that we are to go and do the same as the one who showed mercy to the man who had a physical need. We are supposed to have mercy on the needy. Almost everyone that I have known in church groups are very much against our country providing affordable healthcare for all, so the religious people that I have known are still acting like the 2 religious guys in this example, the priest and the levite. Levites were assistants to the priest. I find it interesting that Jesus would use 2 religious guys in this example that also didn't care to help the injured needy man. How does this example guide us politically? I strongly believe that it should guide the church of today to rethink the healthcare issue, and be like Jesus told us to be. How does your political choice feel about those who need healthcare? Are they loving the people, or the money?

Matthew 10:42 (NASB)

42 And whoever in the name of a disciple gives to one of these little ones even a cup of cold water to drink, truly I say to you, he shall not lose his reward.

Christians should be givers.

Luke 12:13-21 (NASB)
Covetousness Denounced

13 Someone in the crowd said to Him, "Teacher, tell my brother to divide the family inheritance with me." 14 But He said to him, "Man, who appointed Me a judge or arbitrator over you?" 15 Then He said to them, "Beware, and be on your guard against every form of greed; for not **even** when one has an abundance does his life consist of his possessions." 16 And He told them a parable, saying, "The land of a rich man was very productive. 17 And he began reasoning to himself, saying, 'What shall I do, since I have no place to store my crops?' 18 Then he said,

'This is what I will do: I will tear down my barns and build larger ones, and there I will store all my grain and my goods. ¹⁹ And I will say to my soul, "Soul, you have many goods laid up for many years to come; take your ease, eat, drink, and be merry."' ²⁰ But God said to him, 'You fool! This very night your soul is required of you; and now who will own what you have prepared?' ²¹ So is the man who stores up treasure for himself, and is not rich toward God."

Jesus said to "beware, and be on your guard against every form of greed." Being rich toward God as Jesus mentions in verse 21 is important especially if you are wealthy, and being rich toward God is very obviously being generous toward others according to several of our scriptural examples. More tax cuts for the wealthy is very opposite of what Jesus tells the wealthy to do here.

Matthew 12:7 (NASB)

⁷ But if you had known what this means, 'I DESIRE COMPASSION, AND NOT A SACRIFICE,' you would not have condemned the innocent.

True compassion is having deep sympathy and sorrow for another who is stricken by misfortune, accompanied by a strong desire to alleviate the suffering.

Luke 11:37-42 (NASB)
Woes Upon the Pharisees

³⁷ Now when He had spoken, a Pharisee asked Him to have lunch with him; and He went in, and reclined at the table. ³⁸ When the Pharisee saw it, he

was surprised that He had not first ceremonially washed before the meal. [39] But the Lord said to him, "Now you Pharisees clean the outside of the cup and of the platter; but inside of you, you are full of robbery and wickedness. [40] You foolish ones, did not He who made the outside make the inside also? [41] But give that which is within as charity, and then all things are clean for you.

[42] "But woe to you Pharisees! For you pay tithe of mint and rue and every kind of garden herb, and yet disregard justice and the love of God; but these are the things you should have done without neglecting the others.

The Pharisees were a very religious group on the outside, but they were lovers of money, not people. Jesus said they should not have disregarded justice and the love of God. Justice is about doing what is right for the people, which is a major part of loving God. The political parties in the world that love money and take away from the people through all kinds of oppression, I believe have a heart much like the Pharisees did.

Luke 14:12-14 (NASB)

[12] And He also went on to say to the one who had invited Him, "When you give a luncheon or a dinner, do not invite your friends or your brothers or your relatives or rich neighbors, otherwise they may also invite you in return and that will be your repayment. [13] But when you give a reception, invite the poor, the crippled, the lame, the blind, [14] and you will be blessed, since they do not have the means to repay you; for you will be repaid at the resurrection of the righteous."

If you are a Christian politician you should have a special place in your heart for the poor, sick and needy, especially after reading Jesus words from verses like these, and you will be wise to follow Him.

Matthew 19:16-26 (NASB)
The Rich Young Ruler

[16] And someone came to Him and said, "Teacher, what good thing shall I do that I may obtain eternal life?" [17] And He said to him, "Why are you asking Me about what is good? There is only One who is good; but if you wish to enter into life, keep the commandments." [18] Then he said to Him, "Which ones?" And Jesus said, "'YOU SHALL NOT COMMIT MURDER; YOU SHALL NOT COMMIT ADULTERY; YOU SHALL NOT STEAL; YOU SHALL NOT BEAR FALSE WITNESS; [19] HONOR YOUR FATHER AND MOTHER; and YOU SHALL LOVE YOUR NEIGHBOR AS YOURSELF" [20] The young man said to Him, "All these things I have kept; what am I still lacking?" [21] Jesus said to him, "If you wish to be complete, go and sell your possessions and give to the poor, and you will have treasure in heaven; and come, follow Me." [22] But when the young man heard this statement, he went away grieving; for he was one who owned much property. [23] And Jesus said to His disciples, "Truly I say to you, it is hard for a rich man to enter the kingdom of heaven. [24] Again I say to you, it is easier for a camel to go through the eye of a needle, than for a rich man to enter the kingdom of God." [25] When the disciples

heard this, they were very astonished and said, "Then who can be saved?" **26** And looking at them Jesus said to them, "With people this is impossible, but with God all things are possible."

Matthew 23:23-28 (NASB)

23 "Woe to you, scribes and Pharisees, hypocrites! For you tithe mint and dill and cumin, and have neglected the weightier provisions of the law: justice and mercy and faithfulness; but these are the things you should have done without neglecting the others. **24** You blind guides, who strain out a gnat and swallow a camel!

25 "Woe to you, scribes and Pharisees, hypocrites! For you clean the outside of the cup and of the dish, but inside they are full of robbery and self-indulgence. **26** You blind Pharisee, first clean the inside of the cup and of the dish, so that the outside of it may become clean also.

27 "Woe to you, scribes and Pharisees, hypocrites! For you are like whitewashed tombs which on the outside appear beautiful, but inside they are full of dead men's bones and all uncleanness. **28** So you, too, outwardly appear righteous to men, but inwardly you are full of hypocrisy and lawlessness.

Jesus was very against the Pharisees robbery and self-indulgence. Jesus said they should have had justice and mercy and faithfulness, and in the context of this scripture, it once again is really about loving our neighbor as ourself and loving people more than money, which equates scripturally to loving God. Which political party do you believe is loving God most with treating the people with justice and mercy and faithfulness? It is the party that loves money the least.

Luke 16:19-31 (NASB)
The Rich Man and Lazarus

[19] "Now there was a rich man, and he habitually dressed in purple and fine linen, joyously living in splendor every day. [20] And a poor man named Lazarus was laid at his gate, covered with sores, [21] and longing to be fed with the crumbs which were falling from the rich man's table; besides, even the dogs were coming and licking his sores. [22] Now the poor man died and was carried away by the angels to Abraham's bosom; and the rich man also died and was buried. [23] In Hades he lifted up his eyes, being in torment, and saw Abraham far away and Lazarus in his bosom. [24] And he cried out and said, 'Father Abraham, have mercy on me, and send Lazarus so that he may dip the tip of his finger in water and cool off my toungue, for I am in agony in this flame.' [25] But Abraham said, 'Child, remember that during your life you received your good things, and likewise Lazarus bad things; but now he is being comforted here, and you are in agony. [26] And besides all this, between us and you there is a great chasm fixed, so that those who wish to come over from here to you will not be able, and that none may cross over from there to us.' [27] And he said, 'Then I beg you, father, that you send him to my father's house- [28] for I have five brothers- in order that he may warn them, so that they will not also come to this place of torment.' [29] But Abraham said, 'They have Moses and the Prophets; let them hear them.' [30] But he said, 'No, father Abraham, but if someone goes to them from the dead, they will

repent!' **31** But he said to him, 'If they do not listen to Moses and the Prophets, they will not be persuaded even if someone rises from the dead.

Do you think Jesus would tell us a story like this to make us care less about the poor, and more about the wealthy? Think about it. The people are much more important than the money. True biblical Christianity is concerned for the needs of all.

John 13:34-35 (NASB)

34 A new commandment I give to you, that you love one another, even as I have loved you, that you also love one another. **35** By this all men will know that you are My disciples, if you have love for one another."

Which political party is loving the people more? The party that wants to give very affordable healthcare for all, by taxing the wealthy a little more and by cutting war spending, or the party that cuts services that help the sick poor and needy to give more tax cuts to the wealthy and more war spending? Which is loving the people more?

John 15:12-17 (NASB)
Disciples' Relation to Each Other

12 "This is My commandment, that you love one another, just as I have loved you. **13** Greater love has no one than this, that one lay down his life for his friends. **14** You are My friends if you do what I command you. **15** No longer do I call you slaves, for the slave does not know what his master is doing; but I have called you friends, for all things that I have heard from My Father I have made known to you. **16** You did not choose Me but I chose you, and

appointed you that you would go and bear fruit, and
that your fruit would remain, so that whatever you
ask of the Father in My name He may give to you.
¹⁷ This I command you, that you love one another.

Loving one another is the political opposite of loving money.

Mark 12:41-44 (NASB)
The Widow's Mite

⁴¹ And He sat down opposite the treasury, and began
observing how the people were putting money into
the treasury; and many rich people were putting in
large sums. ⁴² A poor widow came and put in two
small copper coins, which amount to a cent. ⁴³
Calling His disciples to Him, He said to them,
"Truly I say to you, this poor widow put in more
than all the contributors to the treasury; ⁴⁴ for they
all put in out of their surplus, but she, out of her
poverty, put in all she owned, all she had to live
on."

If you are a proclaimed Christian politician, you should be against a tax
system that taxes the middle class at a higher percentage of their income than the
wealthy. Jesus makes it clear that a tiny amount of money means more to the poor
than a great deal of money to the rich. Which political party is responsible for
cutting taxes continually on the wealthy while cutting services that help the needy
to do so? This is not true biblical Christianity.

John 21:15-17 (NASB)
The Love Motivation

¹⁵ So when they had finished breakfast, Jesus said to
Simon Peter, "Simon, son of John, do you love Me

more than these?" he said to Him, "Yes, Lord; You know that I love You." He said to him, "Tend My lambs." **16** He said to him again a second time, "Simon, son of John, do you love Me?" He said to Him, "Yes, Lord; You know that I love You." He said to him, "Shepherd My sheep." **17** He said to him the third time, "Simon, son of John, do you love Me?" Peter was grieved because he said to him the third time, "Do you love Me?" And he said to Him, "Lord, You know all things; You know that I love You." Jesus said, to him, "Tend My sheep."

If you really do love Jesus, you will also love people by your actions. If you're a Christian politician, you need to start heeding Jesus words regarding holding people in a much higher place than more tax cuts for the wealthy. Are you telling us that you're a Christian politician? Then start tending Jesus sheep by letting go of the money and tending to the needs of the people.

Matthew 4:8-11 (NASB)
8 Again, the devil took Him to a very high mountain and showed Him all the kingdoms of the world and their glory; **9** and he said to Him, "All these things I will give You, if You fall down and worship me." **10** Then Jesus said to him, "Go, Satan! For it is written, 'You shall worship the Lord your God, and serve him only.'" **11** Then the devil left Him; and behold, angels came and began to minister to Him.

So what do you believe Jesus meant when He said "You shall worship the Lord your God, and serve Him only? Which master do you think Jesus was here to serve? God, by loving and serving the people, or money, by serving His own interest? Remember, you can't serve them both, its one or the other. Jesus was sent here to serve all of mankind, He had to make all of the right decisions, to do the right thing, for all of the people. Yes, He was sent by God the father, for the benefit of the people. He was not sent here for His own satisfaction, or for His own pleasure, but He was sent here to do a really big job for all of the people. Jesus was faced here by the devil in the wilderness, after 40 days and 40 nights of fasting. Jesus had to be very weak physically at that time, and very vulnerable to temptation. The biblical ruler of this present world is Satan, and as it says here, the devil had power to give Jesus all the Kingdoms of the world, and their glory. When the devil offered them all to Jesus for the cost of Jesus falling down and worshipping him, Jesus knew better than that, and he sharply rebuked the devil, and resisted him with the word of God. Jesus knew He was here to serve God the father, and that meant He was here to serve the people's best interest. Though the devil probably did have at the very least, every monetary thing that the world had to offer to Jesus.

Sound familiar politically? Maybe it should! A very similar scenario faces our politicians. Our politicians are sent into their positions of power to do the best job that they can do for the people. But far too often the politicians bow down to their corporate lobbyist masters, who supply them with lots of money and things of pleasure, to do what is almost always going to hurt the poor, needy, hungry, helpless, orphan, afflicted, widow, fatherless, alien, (immigrant) stranger and all who are oppressed. How sad this is, especially when the politician who takes money from the corporation, in opposition to the people's best interest, was voted in, claiming to be a Christian, while the needs of the needy continue to grow, and the rich's of the corporate elite, continue to prosper more than ever. Do you believe that these corporate self-serving politicians who take money to vote against the people's best interest are serving and loving God, by loving their neighbor as themselves?

Matthew 6:19-21 (NASB)

[19] "Do not store up for yourselves treasures on earth, where moth and rust destroy, and where thieves break in and steal. [20] But store up for

yourselves treasures in heaven, where neither moth
nor rust destroys, and where thieves do not break in
or steal; [21] *for where your treasure is, there your*
heart will be also.

This passage is about people and money again, and when you speak politically, your words clearly identify and make evident, which is most important to you.

Matthew 7:7-12 (NASB)
Prayer and the Golden Rule

[7] "Ask, and it will be given to you; seek, and you will find; knock, and it will be opened to you. [8] For everyone who asks receives, and he who seeks finds, and to him who knocks it will be opened. [9] Or what man is there among you who, when his son asks for a loaf, will give him a stone? [10] Or if he asks for a fish, he will not give him a snake, will he? [11] If you then, being evil, know how to give good gifts to your children, how much more will your Father who is in heaven give what is good to those who ask Him!
[12] "In everything, therefore, treat people the same way you want them to treat you, for this is the Law and the Prophets.

God is a huge giver and we should have that same mindset if we are truly His children. When Jesus said "In everything, therefore, treat people the same way you want them to treat you, for this is the law and the prophets." How do you believe this scripture relates to political subjects like affordable healthcare for all thru government? Should you be concerned about the poor person that can't afford the medical treatment he, she or their children so desperately need, or is it more fitting as a Christian as far as you're concerned to want nothing to do with helping these people and looking at them as a burden?

Matthew 7:13-14 (NASB)
The Narrow and Wide Gates

[13]"Enter through the narrow gate; for the gate is wide and the way is broad that leads to destruction, and there are many who enter through it. [14] For the gate is small and the way is narrow that leads to life, and there are few who find it.

Matthew 11:16-19 (NASB)

[16] "But to what shall I compare this generation? It is like children sitting in the market places, who call out to the other children, [17] and say, 'We played the flute for you, and you did not dance; we sang a dirge, and you did not mourn.' [18] For John came neither eating nor drinking, and they say, 'He has a demon!' [19] The Son of Man came eating and drinking, and they say, 'Behold, a gluttonous man and a drunkard, a friend of tax collectors and sinners!' Yet wisdom is vindicated by her deeds."

There are so many half-truths told by politicians, but does the politicians' words line up with how they voted on the bills of law? The guilty say many nasty things against the innocent, but politically, the bottom line is how they vote on the bills that affect the nation's people. This is what we need to pay attention to more than believing the politicians' words. As Jesus said "Wisdom is vindicated by her deeds."

Matthew 12:33-37 (NASB)
Words Reveal Character
[33] "Either make the tree good and its fruit good, or make the tree bad and its fruit bad; for the tree is known by its fruit. [34] You brood of vipers, how can you, being evil, speak what is good? For the mouth speaks out of that which fills the heart. [35] The good man brings out of his good treasure what is good; and the evil man brings out of his evil treasure what is evil. [36] But I tell you that every careless word that people speak, they shall give an accounting for it in the day of judgment. [37] For by your words you will be justified, and by your words you will be condemned."

Is the politician talking about cutting services that help the needy? Is he talking about deregulating big corporations? Or the opposite? These matters show the heart.

Matthew 14:15-16 (NASB)
[15] When it was evening, the disciples came to Him and said, "This place is desolate and the hour is already late; so send the crowds away, that they may go into the villages and buy food for themselves." [16] But Jesus said to them, "They do not need to go away; you give them something to eat!"

Yes Jesus demonstrates a great miracle of feeding the thousands with the few loaves and fishes, but I show this scripture example to show Jesus as very generous. Sure He could do the miracle, but he still had to be there at that place much longer then if he had just sent them home right away. He was also probably tired enough at that time of day. Jesus is generous and so should we be as a people, especially if you want to call yourself a Christian.

Matthew 16:24-27 (NASB)
Discipleship Is Costly

24 Then Jesus said to His disciples, "If anyone wishes to come after Me, he must deny himself, and take up his cross and follow Me. 25 For whoever wishes to save his life will lose it; but whoever loses his life for My sake will find it. 26 For what will it profit a man if he gains the whole world and forfeits his soul? Or what will a man give in exchange for his soul? 27 For the Son of Man is going to come in the glory of His Father with His angels, and WILL THEN REPAY EVERY MAN ACCORDING TO HIS DEEDS.

In knowing that Jesus cares for people so very much, this example that He gives is very sobering if you are a voter and especially a law maker in regard to the poor, sick, and needy.

Matthew 17:24-27 (NASB)
The Tribute Money

24 When they came to Capernaum, those who collected the two-drachma **tax** came to Peter and said, "Does your teacher not pay the two-drachma **tax?**" 25 He said, "Yes." And when he came into the house, Jesus spoke to him first, saying, "What do you think, Simon? From whom do the kings of the earth collect customs or poll-tax, from their sons or from strangers?" 26 When Peter said, "From strangers," Jesus said to him, "Then the sons are exempt. 27 However, so that we do not offend them, go to the sea and throw in a hook, and take the first

fish that comes up; and when you open its mouth, you will find a shekel. Take that and give it to them for you and Me."

Jesus paid tax in order not to offend them. He did not question them, or argue about government spending.

Matthew 24:4-5 (NASB)

[4] And Jesus answered and said to them, "See to it that no one misleads you. [5] For many will come in My name, saying, 'I am the Christ,' and will mislead many.

Matthew 24:11-14 (NASB)

[11] Many false prophets will arise and will mislead many. [12] Because lawlessness is increased, most people's love will grow cold. [13] But the one who endures to the end, he will be saved. [14] This gospel of the kingdom shall be preached in the whole world as a testimony to all the nations, and then the end will come.

Jesus said "Many false prophets will arise and will mislead many because lawlessness is increased, most people's love will grow cold." Are you a Christian pastor or politician who votes against a government that helps the poor, needy, hungry, helpless, orphan, afflicted, widow, fatherless, alien (immigrant) stranger and all who are oppressed by the oppressors?

Mark 7:1-23 (NASB)
Followers of Tradition

[1] The Pharisees and some of the scribes gathered

around Him when they had come from Jerusalem, [2] and had seen that some of His disciples were eating their bread with impure hands, that is, unwashed. [3] (For the Pharisees and all the Jews do not eat unless they carefully wash their hands, *thus* observing the traditions of the elders; [4] and *when they come* from the market place, they do not eat unless they cleanse themselves; and there are many other things which they have received in order to observe, such as the washing of cups and pitchers and copper pots.) [5] The Pharisees and the scribes *asked Him, "Why do Your disciples not walk according to the tradition of the elders, but eat their bread with impure hands?" [6] And He said to them, "Rightly did Isaiah prophesy of you hypocrites, as it is written: 'THIS PEOPLE HONORS ME WITH THEIR LIPS, BUT THEIR HEART IS FAR AWAY FROM ME. [7] 'BUT IN VAIN DO THEY WORSHIP ME, TEACHING AS DOCTRINES THE PRECEPTS OF MEN.' [8] Neglecting the commandment of God, you hold to the tradition of men."

[9] He was also saying to them, "You are experts at setting aside the commandment of God in order to keep your tradition. [10] For Moses said, 'HONOR YOUR FATHER AND YOUR MOTHER'; and, 'HE WHO SPEAKS EVIL OF FATHER OR MOTHER, IS TO BE PUT TO DEATH'; [11] but you say, 'If a man says to *his* father or *his* mother, whatever I have that would help you is Corban (that is to say, given *to God*),' [12] you no longer permit

him to do anything for *his* father
or *his* mother; [13] *thus* invalidating the word of God
by your tradition which you have handed down; and
you do many things such as that."

The Heart of Man

[14] After He called the crowd to Him again,
He *began* saying to them, "Listen to Me, all of you,
and understand: [15] there is nothing outside the man
which can defile him if it goes into him; but the
things which proceed out of the man are what defile
the man. [16] [If anyone has ears to hear, let him
hear."]

[17] When he had left the crowd and entered the
house, His disciples questioned Him about the
parable. [18] And He said to them, "Are you so lacking
in understanding also? Do you not understand that
whatever goes into the man from outside cannot
defile him, [19] because it does not go into his heart,
but into his stomach, and is eliminated?" (Thus He
declared all foods clean.) [20] And He was
saying, "That which proceeds out of the man, that is
what defiles the man.[21] For from within, out of the
heart of men, proceed the evil
thoughts, fornications, thefts, murders,
adulteries,[22] deeds of coveting *and* wickedness, as
well as deceit, sensuality, envy,
slander, pride *and* foolishness. [23] All these evil
things proceed from within and defile the man."

Jesus is emphasizing that our religiousness doesn't mean anything, but
again gives an example of how these religious people chose money even over

their own parents in verses 10-13. Jesus also states that nothing that goes into the mouth makes a person unclean, but only what proceeds out of the mouth can defile a man.

> **Luke 6:20-26 (NASB)**
> **The Beatitudes**
> [20] And turning His gaze toward His disciples, He began to say, "Blessed are you who are poor, for yours is the kingdom of God. [21] Blessed are you who hunger now, for you shall be satisfied. Blessed are you who weep now, for you shall laugh. [22] Blessed are you when men hate you, and ostracize you, and insult you, and scorn your name as evil, for the sake of the Son of Man. [23] Be glad in that day and leap for joy, for behold, your reward is great in heaven. For in the same way their fathers used to treat the prophets. [24] But Woe to you who are rich, for you are receiving your comfort in full. [25] Woe to you who are well-fed now, for you shall be hungry. Woe to you who laugh now, for you shall mourn and weep. [26] Woe to you when all men speak well of you, for their fathers used to treat the false prophets in the same way.

Some very sobering words for the politicians who spend all of their efforts serving themselves and the rich.

> **Luke 12:1-5 (NASB)**
> **God Knows and Cares**
> [1] Under these circumstances, after so many thousands of people had gathered together that they were stepping on one another, He began saying to

His disciples first of all, "Beware of the leaven of the Pharisees, which is hypocrisy. [2] But there is nothing covered up that will not be revealed, and hidden that will not be known. [3] Accordingly, whatever you have said in the dark will be heard in the light, and what you have whispered in the inner rooms will be proclaimed upon the housetops. [4] "I say to you, My friends, do not be afraid of those who kill the body and after that have no more that they can do. [5] But I will warn you whom to fear: fear the One who, after He has killed, has authority to cast into hell; yes, I tell you, fear Him!

John 15:12 (NASB)
Disciples' Relation to Each Other
[12] "This is My commandment, that you love one another, just as I have loved you.

Matthew 7:15-29 (NASB)
A Tree and Its Fruit
[15] "Beware of the false prophets, who come to you in sheep's clothing, but inwardly are ravenous wolves. [16] You will know them by their fruits. Grapes are not gathered from thorn bushes nor figs from thistles, are they? [17] So every good tree bears good fruit, but the bad tree bears bad fruit. [18] A good tree cannot produce bad fruit, nor can a bad tree produce good fruit. [19] Every tree that does not bear good fruit is cut down and thrown into the fire. [20] So then, you will know them by their fruits.

[21] "Not everyone who says to Me, 'Lord, Lord,' will enter the kingdom of heaven, but he who does the will of My Father who is in heaven will enter. [22] Many will say to Me on that day, 'Lord, Lord, did we not prophesy in Your name, and in Your name cast out demons, and in Your name perform many miracles?' [23] And then I will declare to them, 'I never knew you; DEPART FROM ME, YOU WHO PRACTICE LAWLESSNESS.'

The Two Foundations

[24] "Therefore everyone who hears these words of Mine and acts on them, may be compared to a wise man who built his house on the rock. [25] And the rain fell, and the floods came, and the winds blew and slammed against that house; and yet it did not fall, for it had been founded on the rock. [26] Everyone who hears these words of Mine and does not act on them, will be like a foolish man who built his house on the sand. [27] The rain fell, and the floods came, and the winds blew and slammed against that house; and it fell—and great was its fall." [28] When Jesus had finished these words, the crowds were amazed at His teaching; [29] for He was teaching them as one having authority, and not as their scribes.

Jesus said "You will know them by their fruits." He did not say that we would know them by who they say that they are. We will end the Jesus portion of this book with Matthew 25:31-46 again to recap a good example of what some of the fruits are.

Matthew 25:31-46 (NASB)

The Judgment

[31] "But when the Son of Man comes in His glory, and all the angels with Him, then He will sit on His glorious throne. [32] All the nations will be gathered before Him; and He will separate them from one another, as the shepherd separates the sheep from the goats; [33] and He will put the sheep on His right, and the goats on the left.

[34] "Then the King will say to those on His right, 'Come, you who are blessed of My Father, inherit the kingdom prepared for you from the foundation of the world. [35] For I was hungry, and you gave Me something to eat; I was thirsty, and you gave Me something to drink; I was a stranger, and you invited Me in; [36] naked, and you clothed Me; I was sick, and you visited Me; I was in prison, and you came to Me.' [37] Then the righteous will answer Him, 'Lord, when did we see You hungry, and feed You, or thirsty, and give You something to drink? [38] And when did we see You a stranger, and invite You in, or naked, and clothe You? [39] When did we see You sick, or in prison, and come to You?' [40] The King will answer and say to them, 'Truly I say to you, to the extent that you did it to one of these brothers of Mine, even the least of them, you did it to Me.'

[41] "Then He will also say to those on His left, 'Depart from Me, accursed ones, into the eternal fire which has been prepared for the devil and his angels; [42] for I was hungry, and you gave Me nothing to eat; I was thirsty, and you gave Me

nothing to drink; [43] I was a stranger, and you did not
invite Me in; naked, and you did not clothe Me;
sick, and in prison, and you did not visit
Me.' [44] Then they themselves also will answer,
'Lord, when did we see You hungry, or thirsty, or a
stranger, or naked, or sick, or in prison, and did
not take care of You?' [45] Then He will answer them,
'Truly I say to you, to the extent that you did not do
it to one of the least of these, you did not do it to
Me.' [46] These will go away into eternal punishment,
but the righteous into eternal life."

Which side of Jesus does your life's choices put you on? Which side are
you more likened to? Which side is your political party more likened to?

CHAPTER FIVE
Earliest Christian Church Government, Shortly Following Christ Departure and Ascension

Something to Consider

The book of Acts is about the early Christian church, led by the original disciples (apostles) of Jesus, who had personally walked with Jesus, learned from Jesus, and basically lived with Jesus for about 3 years. These people had first-hand teachings from Jesus, the head and master of Christianity Himself. If we want to know what the Christian church should look like, we will not find a more original example then here in the book of Acts. The scripture examples given here, are shortly after Christ departure and ascension. The next 2 scripture examples show us how all of the property, possessions, land and houses of the early Christian people, were actually governed by the church apostles, shared by all, and distributed to each as any had need.

Acts 2:44-47 (NASB)

[44] And all those who had believed were together
and had all things in common; [45] and
they began selling their property and possessions
and were sharing them with all, as anyone might
have need. [46] Day by day continuing with one mind
in the temple, and breaking bread from house to
house, they were taking their meals together with
gladness and sincerity of heart, [47] praising God
and having favor with all the people. And the
Lord was adding to their number day by day those
who were being saved.

Acts 4:32-35 (NASB)
Sharing Among Believers
[32] And the congregation of those who believed were
of one heart and soul; and not one of them claimed
that anything belonging to him was his own, but all
things were common property to them. [33] And with
great power the apostles were giving testimony to
the resurrection of the Lord Jesus, and abundant
grace was upon them all. [34] For there was not a
needy person among them, for all who were owners
of land or houses would sell them and bring
the proceeds of the sales [35] and lay them at the
apostles' feet, and they would be distributed to each
as any had need.

Not one of them claimed that anything belonging to him was his own, but all things were common property to them. For there was not a needy person among them, for all who were owners of land or houses would sell them and bring the proceeds of the sales, and lay them at the apostles feet, and they would be distributed to each as any had need. Please, please read these last 2 scripture examples from Acts chapters 2 and 4 over and over and over, until you understand, that true biblical Christianity is not conservative at all, when it comes to the cost and value of social justice and human rights, because true biblical Christianity eliminates the needs of all, and does it without complaining about what it will cost. These early Christians taught by Jesus, gave up their thoughts of ownership with everything they had, to share with all, and in their obedience to Christ, they eliminated the needs of all people. We must first understand, that the early Christian church basically governed all of the people's possessions. This is the needless heavenly Christian church that Jesus started, and left for the world to see, not a selfish church, but a selfless church. So the early church gave everything to eliminate need, and today's American church not only does not pay tax into our government to help the needy, but much of the church is against supporting things like affordable healthcare for all people. To me, this is a completely opposite mindset between the early church, and the one that fights the poor today. Here is what happened in the early church to one couple who quietly thought they could get out of giving all that they had for the common good of all people.

Acts 5:1-11

New American Standard Bible (NASB)

Fate of Ananias and Sapphira

[1] But a man named Ananias, with his wife Sapphira, sold a piece of property, [2] and kept back some of the price for himself, with his wife's full knowledge, and bringing a portion of it, he laid it at the apostles' feet. [3] But Peter said, "Ananias, why has Satan filled your heart to lie to the Holy Spirit and to keep back some of the price of the land? [4] While it remained unsold, did it not remain your own? And after it was sold, was it not under your control? Why is it that you have conceived this deed in your heart? You have not lied to men but to God." [5] And as he heard these words, Ananias fell down and breathed his last; and great fear came over all who heard of it. [6] The young men got up and covered him up, and after carrying him out, they buried him.

[7] Now there elapsed an interval of about three hours, and his wife came in, not knowing what had happened. [8] And Peter responded to her, "Tell me whether you sold the land for such and such a price?" And she said, "Yes, that was the

price." ⁹ Then Peter said to her, "Why is it that you
have agreed together to put the Spirit of the Lord to
the test? Behold, the feet of those who have buried
your husband are at the door, and they will carry
you out as well." ¹⁰ And immediately she fell at his
feet and breathed her last, and the young men came
in and found her dead, and they carried her out and
buried her beside her husband. ¹¹ And great fear
came over the whole church, and over all who
heard of these things.

How many like-minded Ananias and Sapphiras fill America's church
congregations today, including many pastors and teachers? How many of these
people who are valuing their money over the healthcare needs among many other
needs of the people, would also collapse and fall to their death before Peter to be
buried? As a Christian who believes your bible, it should be disturbing for you to
see people that are in need of basic things such as healthcare among others. We
have now read about Jesus coming back to judge the nations in regard to how we
treated the people including the least of them in Matthew 25:31-46. We have read
the importance of loving our neighbor as ourself in the greatest commandment of
all. We have read that you can't serve 2 masters, you can't serve God (people) and
money, you must choose one. And, now the scriptures here from the book of Acts
have proven beyond any doubt that if you are a Christian politician or Christian
voter, you should be for, and in complete support of government services such as
Social Security, Medicare, Medicaid, affordable healthcare for all people, public
education, affordable housing, food stamps, fuel assistance, and any other
government service that assists in making the needs of this group of people as
small as possible. And hopefully eliminating the needs of these, the poor, needy,
hungry, helpless, orphan, afflicted, widow, fatherless, alien (immigrant) stranger,
and all who are oppressed by the oppressors. Since America's church is far too
small financially to care for even the healthcare needs alone of America's some

317,000,000 people, America's Christians should be trying to elect the politicians that care about the government services above that represent some of the concerns of the early church government, which are basic needs of the people.

CHAPTER SIX

Be Imitators of God

God is Love

Love Your Neighbor As Yourself

You Can't Serve God and Money

Godly Governments Unite Everyone to Collectively Eliminate at Very Least, the Basic Needs of All.

Now we have seen absolute biblical evidence which has proven, that if we are professed Christians trying to be true to our faith in what Christ taught the church to do as Christians, we will do our best to try to help those who are less fortunate, by voting to eliminate the needs of the needy. We need good governments that care for the needs of all the people, not just the rich. If you are a professed Christian politician, you need to quit voting against the people who elected you, who need your help. Professed Christian politicians need to stop taking the money from the corporations that take away what is best for the majority of the people. If we are Christian voters, we need to rethink our political positions to see if we are helping the poor, needy, hungry, helpless, orphan, afflicted, widow, fatherless, alien, (immigrant) stranger, and all who are oppressed by the oppressors.

As Christians, we don't want to help the oppressors to oppress the people more, by taking more away from them. Christians shouldn't be a part of the problem of oppression, Christians should be on the side of the political parties that create the solutions against oppression. Not cutting the important social safety nets like Social Security, Medicare, Medicaid, but cutting back on the ridiculous amounts spent for War instead, and raising taxes on the wealthiest people back up to the appropriate levels of old again, that would be more biblically correct. Loving God is in loving people, not money, and verbally insulting the needy isn't loving God, helping them is. If we are loving God by loving His people instead of loving money, we will always be on the right side of every politically relatable bible scripture. Here are several more scriptures for you to consider as you run your political mindset of choices through them. You should have peace while reading scripture, if you have made the right choices.

Proverbs 21:2-3 (NASB)

[2] Every man's way is right in his own eyes,
But the Lord weighs the hearts.
[3] To do righteousness and justice
Is desired by the Lord more than sacrifice.

Proverbs 21:13 (NASB)

[13] He who shuts his ear to the cry of the poor
Will also cry himself and not be answered.

Proverbs 22:1 (NASB)

On Life and Conduct

[22] A good name is to be more desired than great wealth,
Favor is better than silver and gold.

Proverbs 22:9-11 (NASB)

[9] He who is generous will be blessed,
For he gives some of his food to the poor.
[10] Drive out the scoffer, and contention will go out,
Even strife and dishonor will cease.
[11] He who loves purity of heart
And whose speech is gracious, the king is his friend.

Jeremiah 9:23-24 (NASB)

[23] Thus says the Lord, "Let not a wise man boast of his wisdom, and let not the mighty man boast of his might, let not a rich man boast of his riches; [24] but let him who boasts boast of this, that he understands and knows Me, that I am the Lord who exercises lovingkindness, justice and righteousness on earth; for I delight in these things," declares the Lord.

Obadiah 1:15 (NASB)
The Day of the Lord and the Future

[15] "For the day of the Lord draws near on all the nations.
As you have done, it will be done to you.
Your dealings will return on your own head.

As you have done, it will be done to you. Your dealings will return on your own head.

Romans 12:9-10 (AMP)

[9] [Let your] love be sincere (a real thing); hate what is evil [loathe all ungodliness, turn in horror from wickedness], but hold fast to that which is good. [10] Love one another with brotherly affection [as members of one family], giving
precedence and showing honor to one another.

1 Corinthians 10:23-24 (NASB)

[23] All things are lawful, but not all things are profitable. All things are lawful, but not all things edify. [24] Let no one seek his own good, but that of his neighbor.

Galatians 5:14 (NASB)

[14] For the whole Law is fulfilled in one word, in the statement, "YOU SHALL LOVE YOUR NEIGHBOR AS YOURSELF."

Galatians 6:2 (NASB)

[2] Bear one another's burdens, and thereby fulfill the law of Christ.

Ephesians 5:1-10 (AMP)

[1] Therefore be imitators of God [copy Him and follow His example], as well-beloved children [imitate their father].

[2] And walk in love, [esteeming and delighting in one another] as Christ loved us and gave Himself up for us, a slain offering and sacrifice to God [for you, so that it became] a sweet fragrance.

[3] But immorality (sexual vice) and all impurity [of lustful, rich, wasteful living] or greediness must not even be named among you, as is fitting and proper among saints (God's consecrated people).

[4] Let there be no filthiness (obscenity, indecency) nor foolish and sinful (silly and corrupt) talk, nor coarse jesting, which are not fitting or becoming; but instead voice your thankfulness [to God].

[5] For be sure of this: that no person practicing sexual vice or impurity in thought or in life, or one who is covetous [who has lustful desire for the property of others and is greedy for gain]—for he [in effect] is an idolater—has any inheritance in the kingdom of Christ and of God.

[6] Let no one delude and deceive you with empty

excuses and groundless arguments [for these sins],
for through these things the wrath of God comes
upon the sons of rebellion and disobedience.
⁷ So do not associate or be sharers with them.
⁸ For once you were darkness, but now you are light
in the Lord; walk as children of Light [lead the lives
of those native-born to the Light].
⁹ For the fruit (the effect, the product) of the
Light or the Spirit [consists] in every form of kindly
goodness, uprightness of heart, and trueness of life.
¹⁰ And try to learn [in your experience] what is
pleasing to the Lord [let your lives be constant
proofs of what is most acceptable to Him].

Philippians 2:1-4 (AMP)
¹ So by whatever [appeal to you there is in our
mutual dwelling in Christ, by whatever]
strengthening and consoling and encouraging [our
relationship] in Him [affords], by whatever
persuasive incentive there is in love, by whatever
participation in the [Holy] Spirit [we share], and by
whatever depth of affection and compassionate
sympathy,
² Fill up and complete my joy by living in
harmony and being of the same mind and one in
purpose, having the same love, being in full accord
and of one harmonious mind and intention.
³ Do nothing from factional motives [through
contentiousness, strife, selfishness, or for unworthy
ends] or prompted by conceit and empty arrogance.
Instead, in the true spirit of humility (lowliness of
mind) let each regard the others as better

than and superior to himself [thinking more highly of one another than you do of yourselves].

[4] Let each of you esteem and look upon and be concerned for not [merely] his own interests, but also each for the interests of others.

Philippians 2:19-21 (NASB)
Timothy and Epaphroditus

[19] But I hope in the Lord Jesus to send Timothy to you shortly, so that I also may be encouraged when I learn of your condition. [20] For I have no one else of kindred spirit who will genuinely be concerned for your welfare. [21] For they all seek after their own interests, not those of Christ Jesus.

Hebrews 13:1-3 (AMP)

[1] Let love for your fellow believers continue and be a fixed practice with you [never let it fail].

[2] Do not forget *or* neglect *or* refuse to extend hospitality to strangers [in the brotherhood—being friendly, cordial, and gracious, sharing the comforts of your home and doing your part generously], for through it some have entertained angels without knowing it.

[3] Remember those who are in prison as if you were their fellow prisoner, and those who are ill-treated, since you also are liable to bodily sufferings.

James 2:1-9
Amplified Bible (AMP)

[1] My brethren, pay no servile regard to people [show no prejudice, no partiality]. Do not [attempt

to] hold and practice the faith of our Lord Jesus
Christ [the Lord] of glory [together with snobbery]!
² For if a person comes into your congregation
whose hands are adorned with gold rings and who
is wearing splendid apparel, and also a poor [man]
in shabby clothes comes in,
³ And you pay special attention to the one who
wears the splendid clothes and say to him, Sit here
in this preferable seat! while you tell the poor
[man], Stand there! or, Sit there on the floor at my
feet!
⁴ Are you not discriminating among your own and
becoming critics and judges with wrong motives?
⁵ Listen, my beloved brethren: Has not God chosen
those who are poor in the eyes of the world to be
rich in faith and in their position as believers and to
inherit the kingdom which He has promised to
those who love Him?
⁶ But you [in contrast] have insulted (humiliated,
dishonored, and shown your contempt for) the poor.
Is it not the rich who domineer over you? Is it not
they who drag you into the law courts?
⁷ Is it not they who slander and blaspheme that
precious name by which you are
distinguished and called [the name of Christ
invoked in baptism]?
⁸ If indeed you [really] fulfill the royal Law in
accordance with the Scripture, You shall love your
neighbor as [you love] yourself, you do well.
⁹ But if you show servile regard (prejudice,
favoritism) for people, you commit sin and are
rebuked and convicted by the Law as

violators and offenders.

James 2:14-20 (NASB)
Faith and Works
[14] What use is it, my brethren, if someone says he
has faith but he has no works? Can that faith save
him? [15] If a brother or sister is without clothing and
in need of daily food, [16] and one of you says to
them, "Go in peace, be warmed and be filled," and
yet you do not give them what is necessary
for their body, what use is that? [17] Even so faith, if it
has no works, is dead, being by itself.
[18] But someone may well say, "You have faith and I
have works; show me your faith without the works,
and I will show you my faith by my works." [19] You
believe that God is one. You do well; the demons
also believe, and shudder. [20] But are you willing to
recognize, you foolish fellow, that faith without
works is useless?

The politician who calls himself Christian then votes to cut services like Social Security, Medicare, Medicaid, public schools, food stamps, fuel assistance or any other government service that helps the poor, needy, hungry, helpless, orphan, afflicted, widow, fatherless, alien (immigrant) stranger and all who are oppressed or could potentially be, fits right in with this scripture. Your faith should start showing some true biblical Christian fruit.

James 3:17-18 (NASB)
[17] But the wisdom from above is first pure,
then peaceable, gentle, reasonable, full of mercy
and good fruits, unwavering,

without hypocrisy. [18] And the seed whose fruit is
righteousness is sown in peace by those who make
peace.

A Godly government that promotes peace is a government that helps the
poor, needy, hungry, helpless, orphan, afflicted, widow, fatherless, alien
(immigrant) stranger and all who are oppressed, or could potentially be oppressed
without assistance from government. The Christian politician who reads their
bible should understand this very well.

1 Peter 1:14-16 (AMP)
[14] [Live] as children of obedience [to God]; do not
conform yourselves to the evil desires [that
governed you] in your former ignorance [when you
did not know the requirements of the Gospel].
[15] But as the One Who called you is holy, you
yourselves also be holy in all your
conduct and manner of living.
[16] For it is written, You shall be holy, for I am holy.

1 Peter 4:8-10 (NASB)
[8] Above all, keep fervent in your love for one
another, because love covers a multitude of sins. [9]
Be hospitable to one another without complaint. [10]
As each one has received a special gift, employ it in
serving one another as good stewards of the
manifold grace of God.

1 John 2:1-11 (AMP)
[1] My little children, I write you these things so that
you may not violate God's law and sin. But if
anyone should sin, we have an Advocate (One Who

will intercede for us) with the Father—[it is] Jesus Christ [the all] righteous [upright, just, Who conforms to the Father's will in every purpose, thought, and action].

² And He [that same Jesus Himself] is the propitiation (the atoning sacrifice) for our sins, and not for ours alone but also for [the sins of] the whole world.

³ And this is how we may discern [daily, by experience] that we are coming to know Him [to perceive, recognize, understand, and become better acquainted with Him]: if we keep (bear in mind, observe, practice) His teachings (precepts, commandments).

⁴ Whoever says, I know Him [I perceive, recognize, understand, and am acquainted with Him] but fails to keep and obey His commandments (teachings) is a liar, and the Truth [of the Gospel] is not in him.

⁵ But he who keeps (treasures) His Word [who bears in mind His precepts, who observes His message in its entirety], truly in him has the love of and for God been perfected (completed, reached maturity). By this we may perceive (know, recognize, and be sure) that we are in Him:

⁶ Whoever says he abides in Him ought [as a personal debt] to walk and conduct himself in the same way in which He walked and conducted Himself.

⁷ Beloved, I am writing you no new commandment, but an old commandment which you have had from the beginning; the old commandment is the message

which you have heard [the doctrine of salvation through Christ].

⁸ Yet I am writing you a new commandment, which is true (is realized) in Him and in you, because the darkness (moral blindness) is clearing away and the true Light (the revelation of God in Christ) is already shining.

⁹ Whoever says he is in the Light and [yet] hates his brother [Christian, born-again child of God his Father] is in darkness even until now.

¹⁰ Whoever loves his brother [believer] abides (lives) in the Light, and in It or in him there is no occasion for stumbling or cause for error or sin.

¹¹ But he who hates (detests, despises) his brother [in Christ] is in darkness and walking (living) in the dark; he is straying and does not perceive or know where he is going, because the darkness has blinded his eyes.

1 John 2:28-29 (AMP)

²⁸ And now, little children, abide (live, remain permanently) in Him, so that when He is made visible, we may have and enjoy perfect confidence (boldness, assurance) and not be ashamed and shrink from Him at His coming.

²⁹ If you know (perceive and are sure) that He [Christ] is [absolutely] righteous [conforming to the Father's will in purpose, thought, and action], you may also know (be sure) that everyone who does righteously [and is therefore in like manner conformed to the divine will] is born (begotten) of Him [God].

1 John 3:7-12 (AMP)

[7] Boys (lads), let no one deceive and lead you astray. He who practices righteousness [who is upright, conforming to the divine will in purpose, thought, and action, living a consistently conscientious life] is righteous, even as He is righteous.

[8] [But] he who commits sin [who practices evildoing] is of the devil [takes his character from the evil one], for the devil has sinned (violated the divine law) from the beginning. The reason the Son of God was made manifest (visible) was to undo (destroy, loosen, and dissolve) the works the devil [has done].

[9] No one born (begotten) of God [deliberately, knowingly, and habitually] practices sin, for God's nature abides in him [His principle of life, the divine sperm, remains permanently within him]; and he cannot practice sinning because he is born (begotten) of God.

[10] By this it is made clear who take their nature from God and are His children and who take their nature from the devil and are his children: no one who does not practice righteousness [who does not conform to God's will in purpose, thought, and action] is of God; neither is anyone who does not love his brother (his fellow believer in Christ).

[11] For this is the message (the announcement) which you have heard from the first, that we should love one another,

[12] [And] not be like Cain who [took his nature and got his motivation] from the evil one and slew his

brother. And why did he slay him? Because his
deeds (activities, works) were wicked and malicious
and his brother's were righteous (virtuous).

Helping the poor and those who have needs is always going to be the right answer.

1 John 3:16-18 (NASB)

[16] We know love by this, that He laid down His life
for us; and we ought to lay down our lives for
the brethren. [17] But whoever has the world's goods,
and sees his brother in need and closes
his heart against him, how does the love of God
abide in him? [18] Little children, let us not love with
word or with tongue, but in deed and truth.

1 John 3:23 (NASB)

[23] This is His commandment, that we believe in the
name of His Son Jesus Christ, and love one another,
just as He commanded us.

1 John 4:7-8 (NASB)

God Is Love

[7] Beloved, let us love one another, for love is from
God; and everyone who loves is born of God
and knows God. [8] The one who does not love does
not know God, for God is love.

If this was the only scripture you had to make your political choice with, it should be enough. Who is more loving of those living on this earth? The Democrats or the Republicans? Or the Liberal or Conservative party in the Nation which you live?

1 John 4:11-13 (NASB)

[11] Beloved, if God so loved us, we also ought to love one another. [12] No one has seen God at any time; if we love one another, God abides in us, and His love is perfected in us. [13] By this we know that we abide in Him and He in us, because He has given us of His Spirit.

Loving people is what God is all about and that's how we know which politicians are most in line with God. Are they trying to solve problems like health-care, and other problems that face the people, or are they always more concerned with what it will cost them? Why are they never concerned with the cost of war?

1 John 4:16-17 (NASB)

[16] We have come to know and have believed the love which God has for us. God is love, and the one who abides in love abides in God, and God abides in him. [17] By this, love is perfected with us, so that we may have confidence in the day of judgment; because as He is, so also are we in this world.

1 John 4:20-21 (NASB)

[20] If someone says, "I love God," and hates his brother, he is a liar; for the one who does not love his brother whom he has seen, cannot love God whom he has not seen. [21] And this commandment we have from Him, that the one who loves God should love his brother also.

3 John 1:5-6 (NASB)

[5] Beloved, you are acting faithfully in whatever you accomplish for the brethren, and especially when they are strangers; [6] and they have testified to your

love before the church. You will do well to send
them on their way in a manner worthy of God.

3 John 1:11 (NASB)
[11] Beloved, do not imitate what is evil, but what is
good. The one who does good is of God; the one
who does evil has not seen God.

Here are some of the traits of true Christianity which you have just read about in Chapter 6.
- Being generous and sharing with the poor.

- Not shutting our ear to the cry of the poor.

- Doing righteousness and justice.

- Bearing one another's burdens and thereby fulfilling the law of Christ.

- Honoring one another above ourselves.

- Seek not our own good but that of our neighbor.

- Love your neighbor as yourself.

- Greed must not even be named among us.

- Do nothing from selfishness, regard one another as more important than ourselves.

- Do not merely look out for our own personal interest but also for the interest of others.

- Do not neglect to show hospitality to strangers.

- Be hospitable to one another without complaint.

Which of your political parties do you feel is doing a better job of this, as they all have some self-proclaimed Christians.

The (More Liberal) Democrat Way of Governing the People's Money.
Tax the wealthiest 1% of Americans adequately enough

AND

Spend less on defense for war

In order for America to provide its people:

• Very affordable healthcare for all people, keep Medicare and Medicaid strong.

• Keep Social Security strong, keep retirement age 62.

• Well-funded quality public schools, quality teachers, books, sports

• Well-funded city bus lines, subways, inexpensive public transportation for all.

• Well-funded city parks and public libraries.

• Well-funded street, highway, and bridge repair to keep roads smooth and safe.

• Well-funded public utility works, lights, water, sewer, snow removal, grass cutting, etc.

• Well-funded police and fire protection for all.

• Well-funded continued research in alternative clean energy sources such as solar, wind & others such as electric vehicles to create jobs and become less reliant on fossil fuels.

• Well-funded E.P.A. Environmental Protection Agency to help ensure clean air and water for all through government regulation of corporate polluters, to keep them honest and to keep pollution to the lowest levels possible.

• Well-funded food inspection.

• Well-funded assistance for food stamps and heat assistance for the poor, many who work.

The Conservative Republican Way of Governing the People's Money.

Reduce taxes on the wealthiest 1% as much as possible

AND

Spend more on defense for war

By cutting funding to government services for the people such as:

• Cut Medicare and Medicaid

• Cut Social Security and raise the retirement age

• Cut public education, schools, teachers, books, sports

• Cut funding to bus lines and affordable public transportation

• Cut funding to city parks and public libraries

• Cut street, highway and bridge repair

• Cut public utility works

• Cut police officers and firefighters

• Cut research in alternative clean energy sources such as solar, wind, and electric vehicles

• Cut E.P.A. Environmental Protection Agency and deregulate corporations to freely pollute the air and water keeping pollution on the rise, making some water undrinkable and air dangerous to breath.

• Cut food inspection

• Cut assistance for food stamps and heat assistance for the poor, many of whom work.

Other Differences About Democrats

(No corporate (for profit) control of government)

- Keep police and firefighters government controlled and not owned and operated by for profit corporations.

- Keep prisons government operated and not owned and operated by for profit corporations.

- Keep our 238 year old postal system government operated and not owned and operated by for profit corporations because it's never taken any tax dollars to operate.

- Keep government regulation of banks for the protection of the people to keep banks accountable and honest, also keeping the FDIC to ensure most peoples' savings in banks are safe.

- Keep sex education and abstinence training and regulate insurers to provide contraception to attempt to keep abortions and unwanted pregnancies to a minimum.

- Let immigrants become citizens, work, and pay tax to help the economy.

- Keep unions strong to give working people the strong voice of collective bargaining against corporate greed.

- In favor of the National Labor Relations Board for the American worker to have rights.

- Keep jobs in America instead of shipping them overseas.

- Strengthen the Voting Rights Act of 1965 to keep voting rights for all people fair, easy and strong. No difficult forms of ID required. Keep accessible same day registration. Make voting faster and easier to keep length of voting lines as short as possible.

- Democrats are very much against the sequester cuts which are not necessary and do nothing but hurt many people along with hurting America's economy.

Other Differences About Republicans

(Allow private corporations to take control of government services for profit)

• Allow private corporations to own and operate police officers and firefighters for profit.

• Allow private (for profit) corporations to own and operate prisons instead of government.

• Allow private corporations to take over America's successful 238 year old postal system for profit.

• Deregulate banks and enable them to be much less accountable for their actions.

• Cut sex education and contraception coverage.

• Spend billions of dollars keeping immigrants illegal and unable to pay tax into our government.

• Get rid of unions and the working people's voice to collectively bargain against corporate greed.

• Not in favor of the National Labor Relations Board for the American worker to have rights.

• In favor of shipping American jobs overseas.

• Weaken the Voting Rights Act of 1965 to make voting more difficult. Harder and more expensive forms of I.D. required. Some ending of accessible same day registration. Longer voting lines are inevitable with the Republican voter ID laws.

• Republicans are in favor of the sequester cuts.

CHAPTER SEVEN
The Poor, Needy, Hungry, Helpless, Orphan, Afflicted, Widow, Fatherless, Alien (Immigrant) Stranger And All Who are Oppressed.

Godly Nations Do the Right Thing for All of the People.

So we have at this point been able to see and understand that good righteous governments where everyone's money works together for the good of all people and helping everyone with providing their needs is something that Jesus is for us doing, and as a direct result of His teaching to His disciples, we have seen that the earliest church was all about making sure that no one was needy, to the point that everyone contributed literally everything they had to share everything with everyone. Now we will look further into the old testament to see God the father's words to or through prophets etc., and also we will look at more new testament scriptures on the poor, needy and afflicted among us, and we will continue to prove beyond any doubt, that the needy have always been of extreme importance to God the father, and our governments across the world should reflect how important the needs of the people being met, are to God. God rewards the nations that follow His commands by making them lenders only to nations, and not borrowers.

Deuteronomy 15:1-11 (NASB)
The Sabbatic Year
[1] "At the end of every seven years you shall grant a remission of debts. [2] This is the manner of remission: every creditor shall release what he has loaned to his neighbor; he shall not exact it of his

neighbor and his brother, because
the Lord's remission has been proclaimed. [3] From a
foreigner you may exact it, but your hand shall
release whatever of yours is with your
brother. [4] However, there will be no poor among
you, since the Lord will surely bless you in the land
which the Lord your God is giving you as an
inheritance to possess, [5] if only you listen
obediently to the voice of the Lord your God, to
observe carefully all this commandment which I am
commanding you today. [6] For the Lord your God
will bless you as He has promised you, and you will
lend to many nations, but you will not borrow; and
you will rule over many nations, but they will not
rule over you.

[7] "If there is a poor man with you, one of your
brothers, in any of your towns in your land which
the Lord your God is giving you, you shall not
harden your heart, nor close your hand from your
poor brother; [8] but you shall freely open your hand
to him, and shall generously lend him sufficient for
his need in whatever he lacks. [9] Beware that there is
no base thought in your heart, saying, 'The seventh
year, the year of remission, is near,' and your eye is
hostile toward your poor brother, and you give him
nothing; then he may cry to the Lord against you,
and it will be a sin in you. [10] You shall generously
give to him, and your heart shall not be grieved
when you give to him, because for this thing
the Lord your God will bless you in all your work
and in all your undertakings. [11] For the poor will

never cease to be in the land; therefore I command
you, saying, 'You shall freely open your hand to
your brother, to your needy and poor in your land.'

Notice that God gives nations that listen to this command a blessing to only be a lending nation and not to have to borrow from any, also to be a ruler over many nations but they will not rule over you. And what was so important to God for us to do as a nation? "You shall freely open your hand to your brother, to your needy and poor in your land."

Deuteronomy 24:14-15 (NASB)
[14] "You shall not oppress a hired servant who is poor
and needy, whether he is one of your countrymen or
one of your aliens who is in your land in
your towns. [15] You shall give him his wages on his
day before the sun sets, for he is poor and sets
his heart on it; so that he will not cry against you to
the Lord and it become sin in you.

I would not want to be the people in charge of nations who try to keep the minimum wage as low as they can to nearly unlivable levels, and always vote against the poor. These are the oppressors in America. How many cries from the poor have come to God because of you?

Deuteronomy 27:19 (NASB)
[19] 'Cursed is he who distorts the justice due an
alien, orphan, and widow.' And all the people shall
say, 'Amen.'

Wise is the politician who hears the Word of God and remembers the Word of God in their every voting decision. Notice the importance of the alien (that's immigrant) and the orphan and widow. The person is cursed who distorts the justice due to them.

Many politicians would argue that nothing is due to anyone unless you're rich. How wrong they will be proven, but it's not too late for them to change yet.

> **Psalm 9:17-18 (NASB)**
> [17] The wicked will return to Sheol,
> Even all the nations who forget God.
> [18] For the needy will not always be forgotten,
> Nor the hope of the afflicted perish forever.

Sheol is a place for the dead, sometimes also referred to as hell, a place that one should seriously do what the word says in trying not to go there. At this point we should know beyond any doubt how important the needy and afflicted are to God, and how he addresses the nations here, in other words, the governments of the nations who should have services in place to serve the afflicted and needy.

> **Psalm 41:1-3 (NASB)**
> **The Psalmist in Sickness Complains of Enemies and False Friends.**
> [1] How blessed is he who considers the helpless;
> The Lord will deliver him in a day of trouble.
> [2] The Lord will protect him and keep him alive,
> And he shall be called blessed upon the earth;
> And do not give him over to the desire of his enemies.
> [3] The Lord will sustain him upon his sickbed;
> In his illness, You restore him to health.

There are several blessings that God gives to those who consider the helpless, and how much greater are these blessings, then the curses that await the greedy.

Psalm 72 (AMP)
[A Psalm] for Solomon.
[1] Give the king [knowledge of] Your [way of] judging, O God, and [the spirit of] Your righteousness to the king's son [to control all his actions].
[2] Let him judge and govern Your people with righteousness, and Your poor and afflicted ones with judgment and justice.
[3] The mountains shall bring peace to the people, and the hills, through [the general establishment of] righteousness.
[4] May he judge and defend the poor of the people, deliver the children of the needy, and crush the oppressor,
[5] So that they may revere and fear You while the sun and moon endure, throughout all generations.
[6] May he [Solomon as a type of King David's greater Son] be like rain that comes down upon the mown grass, like showers that water the earth.
[7] In His [Christ's] days shall the [uncompromisingly] righteous flourish and peace abound till there is a moon no longer.
[8] He [Christ] shall have dominion also from sea to sea and from the River [Euphrates] to the ends of the earth.
[9] Those who dwell in the wilderness shall bow before Him and His enemies shall lick the dust.

[10] The kings of Tarshish and of the coasts shall bring offerings; the kings of Sheba and Seba shall offer gifts.

[11] Yes, all kings shall fall down before Him, all nations shall serve Him.

[12] For He delivers the needy when he calls out, the poor also and him who has no helper.

[13] He will have pity on the poor and weak and needy and will save the lives of the needy.

[14] He will redeem their lives from oppression and fraud and violence, and precious and costly shall their blood be in His sight.

[15] And He shall live; and to Him shall be given gold of Sheba; prayer also shall be made for Him and through Him continually, and they shall bless and praise Him all the day long.

[16] There shall be abundance of grain in the soil upon the top of the mountains [the least fruitful places in the land]; the fruit of it shall wave like [the forests of] Lebanon, and [the inhabitants of] the city shall flourish like grass of the earth.

[17] His name shall endure forever; His name shall continue as long as the sun [indeed, His name continues before the sun]. And men shall be blessed and bless themselves by Him; all nations shall call Him blessed!

[18] Blessed be the Lord God, the God of Israel, Who alone does wondrous things!

[19] Blessed be His glorious name forever; let the whole earth be filled with His glory! Amen and Amen!

[20] The prayers of David son of Jesse are ended.

Notice how important the poor, needy and afflicted are to the righteous King. How important it is to do justice to them.

This is only one of obviously several biblical examples of God's choosing for us to have righteous governments and you can't have righteous governments without helping the needy with your governments.

Look at verse 14 again, you as a leader should know how important it is to also not send precious lives into war. Your profit from war here is very little compared to what trouble might be awaiting you for sending people into war so that you can profit for a little while. Also notice verse 4 showing that a righteous King vindicates the afflicted, saves the children of the needy and crushes the oppressor. The largest oppressors today are the political parties who oppress these people.

Psalm 103:6 (NASB)
[6] The Lord performs righteous deeds
And judgments for all who are oppressed.

And the Lord uses the politicians that understand how important this is to do much of it.
This is how we truly know the Godly from the ungodly politicians, by their deeds, not their words. If they are in line with God's word, these are the most godly of course, and godly governments eliminate poverty in all aspects.

Psalm 146:5-10 (NASB)
[5] How blessed is he whose help is the God of Jacob,
Whose hope is in the Lord his God,
[6] Who made heaven and earth,
The sea and all that is in them;
Who keeps faith forever;
[7] Who executes justice for the oppressed;

Who gives food to the hungry.

The Lord sets the prisoners free.

[8] The Lord opens the eyes of the blind;

The Lord raises up those who are bowed down;

The Lord loves the righteous;

[9] The Lord protects the strangers;

He supports the fatherless and the widow,

But He thwarts the way of the wicked.

[10] The Lord will reign forever,

Your God, O Zion, to all generations.

Praise the Lord!

God uses people to do much of His blessing. Who are the politicians that are listening to God? They are those that help the needy and stop the oppressors.

Proverbs 14:21 (KJV)

[21] He that despiseth his neighbour sinneth.

But he that hath mercy on the poor, happy is he.

Proverbs 14:31 (NKJV)

[31] He who oppresses the poor reproaches his Maker,

But he who honors Him has mercy on the needy.

Proverbs 14:34 (NASB)

[34] Righteousness exalts a nation,

But sin is a disgrace to any people.

By now we should know that a large government supported by enough tax from the wealthiest and enough cuts in War spending to support the poor, needy, hungry, helpless, orphan, afflicted, widow, fatherless, alien, (immigrant) stranger are crucial ingredients of a righteous nation.

Proverbs 16:16-17 (NASB)

[16] How much better it is to get wisdom than gold!

And to get understanding is to be chosen above

silver.

[17] The highway of the upright is to depart from evil;

He who watches his way preserves his life.

Proverbs 22:22-23 (NASB)

[22] Do not rob the poor because he is poor,

Or crush the afflicted at the gate;

[23] For the Lord will plead their case

And take the life of those who rob them.

Politicians take heed and seriously consider doing what is biblically right for the people.

Proverbs 28:27-28 (NASB)

[27] He who gives to the poor will never want,

But he who shuts his eyes will have many curses.

[28] When the wicked rise, men hide themselves;

But when they perish, the righteous increase.

Proverbs 31:8-9 (NASB)

[8] Open your mouth for the mute,

For the rights of all the unfortunate.

[9] Open your mouth, judge righteously,

And defend the rights of the afflicted and needy.

I wish that if a politician calls themselves a Christian, that they would listen to their bible and start caring about the needs of the people. I hate to see Christ's name dragged into the kind of policy making that takes things away from the people, especially the poor, needy, hungry, helpless, orphan, afflicted, widow, fatherless, alien (immigrant) stranger and all who are oppressed. Please start being good to the majority of the people, according to your bible.

Proverbs 31:20 (NASB)
20 She extends her hand to the poor,
And she stretches out her hands to the needy.

This describes the virtuous woman who fears the Lord.

James 1:27 (AMP)
27 External religious worship [religion as it is expressed in outward acts] that is pure and unblemished in the sight of God the Father is this: to visit and help and care for the orphans and widows in their affliction and need, and to keep oneself unspotted and uncontaminated from the world.

This scripture all by itself shows strong biblical support for Medicare, Medicaid and Social Security, which helps millions of people a great deal to stay out of poverty.

Immigration
When I look at all of the kinds of people that God created, I choose to be color blind, when it comes to how I treat everyone, all with equal respect. When the subject of immigration is brought up, I usually wonder how the Kingdom of Heaven will be when it comes to all of God's creation living together in peace. What is your idea of the Kingdom of Heaven? Will we have division among immigrants and strangers, or will everyone be accepted without thought or question? Will there be different classes of people, or will there be unity and

equality of opportunity among us all? Will we have peace with everyone? Will we be charging everyone for our services rendered, or will we be glad to serve one another freely? Will everyone be able to fully use their God given talents without any fear, or will many have to make a poor living doing something that they do not desire to do, just to make ends meet like here, all while their God given talents go to waste?

I believe our short time here is of extreme importance in how we treat people, and has much relevance to the preparation of our eternal future, but of course I am not here to make this case, I am however trying to look at us from an eternal prospective. For example, if it were up to me, I would let immigrants become citizens, get jobs, and pay taxes into our government like the rest of us. Making them stay illegal only creates the opportunity for oppressors to give them a less than acceptable living wage. And spending billions to keep them out plus the loss of their tax dollars not coming into our government is huge. How much of that loss could be spent on education and or healthcare among many other things instead. Question; How many of us who were born in America, are not a result of immigrants? It was my great grandparents who came to America. These next 6 examples continue to support a Godly righteous government as the others have, but these examples also support being good to immigrants, and letting them live free as the rest of us.

Exodus 22:21-27 (NASB)

[21] "You shall not wrong a stranger or oppress him,
for you were strangers in the land of Egypt. [22] You
shall not afflict any widow or orphan. [23] If you
afflict him at all, and if he does cry out to Me, I will
surely hear his cry; [24] and My anger will be kindled,
and I will kill you with the sword, and your wives
shall become widows and your children fatherless.
[25] "If you lend money to My people, to the
poor among you, you are not to act as a creditor to

him; you shall not charge him interest. [26] If you ever take your neighbor's cloak as a pledge, you are to return it to him before the sun sets, [27] for that is his only covering; it is his cloak for his body. What else shall he sleep in? And it shall come about that when he cries out to Me, I will hear him, for I am gracious.

Exodus 23:6-9 (NASB)

[6] "You shall not pervert the justice due to your needy brother in his dispute. [7] Keep far from a false charge, and do not kill the innocent or the righteous, for I will not acquit the guilty.

[8] "You shall not take a bribe, for a bribe blinds the clear-sighted and subverts the cause of the just.

[9] "You shall not oppress a stranger, since you yourselves know the feelings of a stranger, for you also were strangers in the land of Egypt.

Leviticus 19:32-37 (NASB)

[32] 'You shall rise up before the grayheaded and honor the aged, and you shall revere your God; I am the Lord.

[33] 'When a stranger resides with you in your land, you shall not do him wrong. [34] The stranger who resides with you shall be to you as the native among you, and you shall love him as yourself, for you were aliens in the land of Egypt; I am the Lord your God.

[35] 'You shall do no wrong in judgment, in

measurement of weight, or capacity. [36] You shall
have just balances, just weights, a just ephah, and a
just hin; I am the Lord your God, who brought you
out from the land of Egypt. [37] You shall thus observe
all My statutes and all My ordinances and do them;
I am the Lord.'"

Verse 32 makes a good case for Medicare and Medicaid, Social Security and anything that helps the older people financially in the country that you live. Verses 33 and 34 are a strong case for immigration reform, remember Christian politicians, this is your bible.

Numbers 9:14 (GW)
[14] "Foreigners living with you may want to celebrate
the Lord's Passover. They must follow these same
rules and regulations. The same rules will apply to
foreigners and native-born Israelites."

God once again shows the same rules applying to foreigners as natives for celebrating the Lord's Passover.

Deuteronomy 10:12-22 (AMP)
[12] And now, Israel, what does the Lord your God
require of you but [reverently] to fear the Lord your
God, [that is] to walk in all His ways, and to love
Him, and to serve the Lord your God with all your
[mind and] heart and with your entire being,
[13] To keep the commandments of the Lord and His
statutes which I command you today for your good?
[14] Behold, the heavens and the heaven of heavens

belong to the Lord your God, the earth also, with all that is in it and on it.

[15] Yet the Lord had a delight in loving your fathers, and He chose their descendants after them, you above all peoples, as it is this day.

[16] So circumcise the foreskin of your [minds and] hearts; be no longer stubborn and hardened.

[17] For the Lord your God is God of gods and Lord of lords, the great, the mighty, the terrible God, Who is not partial and takes no bribe.

[18] He executes justice for the fatherless and the widow, and loves the stranger or temporary resident and gives him food and clothing.

[19] Therefore love the stranger and sojourner, for you were strangers and sojourners in the land of Egypt.

[20] You shall [reverently] fear the Lord your God; you shall serve Him and cling to Him, and by His name and presence you shall swear.

[21] He is your praise; He is your God, Who has done for you these great and terrible things which your eyes have seen.

[22] Your fathers went down to Egypt seventy persons in all, and now the Lord your God has made you as the stars of the heavens for multitude.

I wish that every congressperson that chose to say they were Christian did not show partiality to those who paid them most to do their bidding, so that they would resemble what true Christianity really is, being good to all people, especially the poor, needy, hungry, helpless, orphan, afflicted, widow, fatherless, alien (immigrant) stranger and all who are oppressed.

Ezekiel 47:21-23

New American Standard Bible (NASB)

[21] "So you shall divide this land among yourselves according to the tribes of Israel. [22] You shall divide it by lot for an inheritance among yourselves and among the aliens who stay in your midst, who bring forth sons in your midst. And they shall be to you as the native-born among the sons of Israel; they shall be allotted an inheritance with you among the tribes of Israel. [23] And in the tribe with which the alien stays, there you shall give **him** his inheritance," declares the Lord GOD.

CHAPTER EIGHT
Scriptures Especially For the Leaders Of the Nations To Consider

Matthew 6:10 (NASB)
10 'Your kingdom come.
Your will be done,
On earth as it is in heaven.'

Every Christian politician and Christian voter should easily recognize and remember this verse from the Lord's Prayer, which of course is part of how the Lord Jesus told us to pray to our heavenly father. "Your kingdom come, your will be done, on earth as it is in heaven." You've probably said these words together many times over the course of your life, but have you ever stopped to think about what these words might actually mean? This verse alone is huge, for all of us, but especially for the politician, in fact, if it were the only direction that we had from God as Christians, what a different world this would be, if we all tried our best to live by it. Can you imagine our decisions being about how we could make this world a little more heavenly for others? Think about it for a minute, even though I realize that we are not in the Promised Land yet. How many things politically would have to change radically for the sake of peace and justice for all, and for the sake of everything to be fair, right and honest? From a biblical standpoint I believe we are still missing even the most basic things that we should be doing as a people, that is, if we think again about Jesus words "Your kingdom come, your will be done, on earth as it is in heaven." The professing Christian politicians that are being true to the bible, are the ones whose goal is always to make everything better for the majority of the people, including the poorest people of all.

So what if all of our professing Christian politicians were to take Jesus words here from the Lord's Prayer seriously? "Your kingdom come, your will be done, on earth as it is in heaven." Well many of them would just about have to change completely the way that they vote on most issues. First of all, heaven will be a perfect place so it's the highest standard to follow, I believe that we all can agree on that. So let's just think about some very simple things, with a heavenly mind. Do you believe that people will be in their best physical condition in heaven, and will it be very inexpensive, like free to feel our best? Then why hasn't every proclaimed Christian intervened in behalf of the people to make everything healthcare related as inexpensive as possible by taking the profit out of healthcare?

Is healthcare a basic need? Yes, so the early church would have made sure this need was taken care of for everyone. "Your kingdom come, your will be done, on earth as it is in heaven." Immigration, will we be worried about immigrants in heaven, and color of skin, or will everyone live in peace together? Will people have to worry about war in heaven and losing loved ones in war? Will people have to worry about getting shot with an assault weapon in heaven? Will big corporate polluters be making lots of pollution in heaven, making some people's air very hazardous to breathe and water undrinkable? Will people who try to care for the planet be criticized by the church, in heaven? It's pretty obvious to realize that what we have here is not very heavenly and does not currently hold up well at all to Jesus words "Your kingdom come, your will be done, on earth as it is in heaven." If Christ were here today as King and ruler of the world, do you think our world would have any destitute villages full of hungry, starving, sick, hopeless people? Of course it wouldn't! So why are we still allowing these terrible detestable things to happen as nations in 2013 and not doing anything substantial about it? God promises to bless the nations that help the poor, yet most of America's leaders are quick to spend the majority of our people's money on defense for more wars, even our leaders who proclaim to be Christian.

Over half of America's budget is spent on defense for more wars, that's more war spending then the next 10 highest countries war spending combined! Meanwhile these same politicians often want to cut things that the majority of the people count on, like education, Social Security, Medicare, and other important things regarding our infrastructure.

Here is a simple fact, a nation that is good to its people when it comes to supplying the basic needs to its people through taxation, will never be righteously proven wrong for doing so with a bible by anyone. If they find one verse against it, there will be many more verses against them. Does the American church know how to discern good political leaders from bad ones? Do we know the difference? If a politician claims to be Christian, what should be more important to him or her, more tax breaks for the rich, or more affordable healthcare for the sick?

You have already conclusively seen that the basic needs of all people should be most important to a Christian politician. It's not difficult to understand why a government such as the early church didn't have any needy people when you consider the fact that everyone gave all, for the benefit of all. I don't doubt that this kind of government may have been the closest type of government to heaven that this world has ever seen, but could America's approximately 350,000 churches today support even the healthcare cost alone of America's 317,000,000 people?

Absolutely not! Not to mention all the other needs of a civilized nation, education, police, fire, roads, environment, and the list goes on. So the church can't do for everyone what it used to do, for all that were in the church, but biblically if you are a Christian, you should want a government that helps with needs just as the early church did, you should be bothered when you see people in need of basics. If America cut our defense spending just a very modest amount, all Americans could have free or very affordable healthcare for starters, and we would still be way ahead of the rest of the world on defense. This alone would greatly lessen the number of poor, needy and afflicted people in America, which would be a giant biblical step in the right direction.

Here are many more politically relatable scriptures in which a politician can find him or herself on one side or the other of the scriptures. It's up to you politicians. Our people are depending on you to do what's right for them, and so is God. I hope these scriptures help you to do the right thing for the majority of the people so that you may live up to Jesus words everyday as well as can be done. "Your kingdom come, your will be done, on earth as it is in heaven." May the bible politics of your every decision, be the right ones for the people, in the sight of God.

Exodus 23:1-2 (AMP)

[1] You SHALL not repeat or raise a false report; you shall not join with the wicked to be an unrighteous witness.
[2] You shall not follow a crowd to do evil; nor shall you bear witness at a trial so as to side with a multitude to pervert justice.

The Christian politician who is being true to God, the bible and the people shall not pervert justice, but will tell the truth and do the right thing for the majority of the people.

Leviticus 19:9-16 (NASB)
Sundry Laws

[9] 'Now when you reap the harvest of your land, you shall not reap to the very corners of your field, nor shall you gather the gleanings of your harvest. [10] Nor shall you glean your vineyard, nor shall you gather the fallen fruit of your vineyard; you shall leave them for the needy and for the stranger. I am the Lord your God.
[11] 'You shall not steal, nor deal falsely, nor lie to one another. [12] You shall not swear falsely by My name, so as to profane the name of your God; I am the Lord.

[13] 'You shall not oppress your neighbor, nor rob him. The wages of a hired man are not to remain with you all night until morning. [14] You shall not curse a deaf man, nor place a stumbling block before the blind, but you shall revere your God; I am the Lord.

[15] 'You shall do no injustice in judgment; you shall not be partial to the poor nor defer to the great, but you are to judge your neighbor fairly. [16] You shall not go about as a slanderer among your people, and you are not to act against the life of your neighbor; I am the Lord.

Deuteronomy 1:16-17 (NASB)

[16] "Then I charged your judges at that time, saying, 'Hear the cases between your fellow countrymen, and judge righteously between a man and his fellow countryman, or the alien who is with him. [17] You shall not show partiality in judgment; you shall hear the small and the great alike. You shall not fear man, for the judgment is God's. The case that is too hard for you, you shall bring to me, and I will hear it.'

Deuteronomy 8:17-18 (GW)

[17] You may say to yourselves, "I became wealthy because of my own ability and strength." [18] But remember the Lord your God is the one who makes you wealthy. He's confirming the promise which he swore to your ancestors. It's still in effect today.

Deuteronomy 16:18-20 (NASB)

[18] "You shall appoint for yourself judges and officers in all your towns which the Lord your God is giving you, according to your tribes, and they shall judge the people with righteous judgment. [19] You shall not distort justice; you shall not be partial, and you shall not take a bribe, for a bribe blinds the eyes of the wise and perverts the words of the righteous. [20] Justice, and only justice, you shall pursue, that you may live and possess the land which the Lord your God is giving you.

Do not distort justice, do not be partial, do not take bribes. Justice and only justice, blessings of God come with this.

Psalm 5:4-6 (NASB)

[4] For You are not a God who takes pleasure in wickedness;
No evil dwells with You.
[5] The boastful shall not stand before Your eyes;
You hate all who do iniquity.
[6] You destroy those who speak falsehood;
The Lord abhors the man of bloodshed and deceit.

The ending of the doers of falsehood bloodshed and deceit doesn't sound good.

Psalm 9:7-12 (NASB)

[7] But the Lord abides forever;
He has established His throne for judgment,
[8] And He will judge the world in righteousness;

He will execute judgment for the peoples with
equity.
[9] The Lord also will be a stronghold for the
oppressed,
A stronghold in times of trouble;
[10] And those who know Your name will put their
trust in You,
For You, O Lord, have not forsaken those who seek
You.
[11] Sing praises to the Lord, who dwells in Zion;
Declare among the peoples His deeds.
[12] For He who requires blood remembers them;
He does not forget the cry of the afflicted.

The Christian politician who is true to their bible will execute judgment
for the people with equity, will be a stronghold for the oppressed, a stronghold in
times of trouble, and will not forget the cry of the afflicted. This politician is
doing God's will on earth.

Psalm 10 (AMP)
[1] Why do You stand afar off, O Lord? Why do You
hide Yourself, [veiling Your eyes] in times of
trouble (distress and desperation)?
[2] The wicked in pride and arrogance hotly
pursue and persecute the poor; let them be taken in
the schemes which they have devised.
[3] For the wicked man boasts (sings the praises) of
his own heart's desire, and the one greedy for gain
curses and spurns, yes, renounces and despises the
Lord.
[4] The wicked one in the pride of his countenance

will not seek, inquire for, and yearn for God; all his thoughts are that there is no God [so He never punishes].

⁵ His ways are grievous [or persist] at all times; Your judgments [Lord] are far above and on high out of his sight [so he never thinks about them]; as for all his foes, he sniffs and sneers at them.

⁶ He thinks in his heart, I shall not be moved; for throughout all generations I shall not come to want or be in adversity.

⁷ His mouth is full of cursing, deceit, oppression (fraud); under his tongue are trouble and sin (mischief and iniquity).

⁸ He sits in ambush in the villages; in hiding places he slays the innocent; he watches stealthily for the poor (the helpless and unfortunate).

⁹ He lurks in secret places like a lion in his thicket; he lies in wait that he may seize the poor (the helpless and the unfortunate); he seizes the poor when he draws him into his net.

¹⁰ [The prey] is crushed, sinks down; and the helpless falls by his mighty [claws].

¹¹ [The foe] thinks in his heart, God has quite forgotten; He has hidden His face; He will never see [my deed].

¹² Arise, O Lord! O God, lift up Your hand; forget not the humble [patient and crushed].

¹³ Why does the wicked [man] condemn (spurn and renounce) God? Why has he thought in his heart, You will not call to account?

¹⁴ You have seen it; yes, You note trouble and grief

(vexation) to requite it with Your hand. The unfortunate commits himself to You; You are the helper of the fatherless.

[15] Break the arm of the wicked man; and as for the evil man, search out his wickedness until You find no more.

[16] The Lord is King forever and ever; the nations will perish out of His land.

[17] O Lord, You have heard the desire and the longing of the humble and oppressed; You will prepare and strengthen and direct their hearts, You will cause Your ear to hear,

[18] To do justice to the fatherless and the oppressed, so that man, who is of the earth, may not terrify them any more.

Examine your ways according to this psalm MR. and MRS. politician. Be the helper of the people, don't be what this psalm describes as wicked. Do yourself and the majority of the people a favor, by doing what is right for them!

Psalm 12 (NASB)
God, a Helper against the Treacherous.
A Psalm of David.

[1] Help, Lord, for the godly man ceases to be,
For the faithful disappear from among the sons of men.

[2] They speak falsehood to one another;
With flattering lips and with a double heart they speak.

[3] May the Lord cut off all flattering lips,
The tongue that speaks great things;

⁴ Who have said, "With our tongue we will prevail;
Our lips are our own; who is lord over us?"
⁵ "Because of the devastation of the afflicted,
because of the groaning of the needy,
Now I will arise," says the Lord; "I will set him in
the safety for which he longs."
⁶ The words of the Lord are pure words;
As silver tried in a furnace on the earth, refined
seven times.
⁷ You, O Lord, will keep them;
You will preserve him from this generation forever.
⁸ The wicked strut about on every side
When vileness is exalted among the sons of men.

God is a helper against the treacherous. Who are the treacherous? Looks like it very well could be those who are working against the afflicted and needy.

Your money is only comforting you for a little longer Mr. and Mrs. Politician. Start doing the right things for these people and yourself. You won't be sorry in the end if you listen to God's word.

Psalm 15 (NASB)
Description of a Citizen of Zion.
A Psalm of David.
¹ O Lord, who may abide in Your tent?
Who may dwell on Your holy hill?
² He who walks with integrity, and works
righteousness,
And speaks truth in his heart.
³ He does not slander with his tongue,
Nor does evil to his neighbor,
Nor takes up a reproach against his friend;

[4] In whose eyes a reprobate is despised,
But who honors those who fear the Lord;
He swears to his own hurt and does not change;
[5] He does not put out his money at interest,
Nor does he take a bribe against the innocent.
He who does these things will never be shaken.

Nor does he take a bribe against the innocent. I will not take another cent from the corporate lobbyist that works against the majority of the people's best interest says the Christian politician who lives as true as possible to their bible.

Psalm 35:10 (NASB)

[10] All my bones will say, "Lord, who is like You,
Who delivers the afflicted from him who is too strong for him,
And the afflicted and the needy from him who robs him?"

Psalm 37:7-21 (NASB)

[7] Rest in the Lord and wait patiently for Him;
Do not fret because of him who prospers in his way,
Because of the man who carries out wicked schemes.
[8] Cease from anger and forsake wrath;
Do not fret; it leads only to evildoing.
[9] For evildoers will be cut off,
But those who wait for the Lord, they will inherit the land.
[10] Yet a little while and the wicked man will be no more;
And you will look carefully for his place and he will not be there.

[11] But the humble will inherit the land

And will delight themselves in abundant prosperity.

[12] The wicked plots against the righteous

And gnashes at him with his teeth.

[13] The Lord laughs at him,

For He sees his day is coming.

[14] The wicked have drawn the sword and bent their bow

To cast down the afflicted and the needy,

To slay those who are upright in conduct.

[15] Their sword will enter their own heart,

And their bows will be broken.

[16] Better is the little of the righteous

Than the abundance of many wicked.

[17] For the arms of the wicked will be broken,

But the Lord sustains the righteous.

[18] The Lord knows the days of the blameless,

And their inheritance will be forever.

[19] They will not be ashamed in the time of evil,

And in the days of famine they will have abundance.

[20] But the wicked will perish;

And the enemies of the Lord will be like the glory of the pastures,

They vanish—like smoke they vanish away.

[21] The wicked borrows and does not pay back,

But the righteous is gracious and gives.

Regarding verse 14 even all by itself should be enough to show you how important it is to vote for the political party that is concerned for the afflicted and needy, and whose policies help them. Notice that those who would vote against helping them would be referred to here as the wicked. Are you voting for the biblically wicked according to this psalm?

Psalm 52 (NASB)
Futility of Boastful Wickedness.
For the choir director. A Maskil of David, when Doeg the Edomite came and told Saul and said to him, "David has come to the house of Ahimelech."

[1] Why do you boast in evil, O mighty man?
The lovingkindness of God endures all day long.

[2] Your tongue devises destruction,
Like a sharp razor, O worker of deceit.

[3] You love evil more than good,
Falsehood more than speaking what is right. Selah.

[4] You love all words that devour,
O deceitful tongue.

[5] But God will break you down forever;
He will snatch you up and tear you away
from your tent,
And uproot you from the land of the living. Selah.

[6] The righteous will see and fear,
And will laugh at him, saying,

[7] "Behold, the man who would not make God his refuge,
But trusted in the abundance of his riches
And was strong in his evil desire."

[8] But as for me, I am like a green olive tree in the house of God;
I trust in the lovingkindness of God forever and ever.

⁹ I will give You thanks forever, because You have
done it,
And I will wait on Your name, for it is good, in the
presence of Your godly ones.

How nice it will be to see the day that these greedy wealthy hoarders of billions who control congress, finally having to pay for all of the oppression and destruction they were happy to bring onto the people, because they loved money much more than the people. Money was their God.

Psalm 68:1-10 (AMP)
To the Chief Musician. A Psalm of David. A song.
¹ God is [already] beginning to arise, and His
enemies to scatter; let them also who hate Him flee
before Him!
² As smoke is driven away, so drive them away; as
wax melts before the fire, so let the wicked perish
before the presence of God.
³ But let the [uncompromisingly] righteous be glad;
let them be in high spirits and glory before God,
yes, let them [jubilantly] rejoice!
⁴ Sing to God, sing praises to His name, cast up a
highway for Him Who rides through the deserts—
His name is the Lord—be in high spirits and glory
before Him!
⁵ A father of the fatherless and a judge and protector
of the widows is God in His holy habitation.
⁶ God places the solitary in families and gives the
desolate a home in which to dwell; He leads the
prisoners out to prosperity; but the rebellious dwell
in a parched land.

[7] O God, when You went forth before Your people,
when You marched through the wilderness—
Selah [pause, and calmly think of that]!—
[8] The earth trembled, the heavens also poured down
[rain] at the presence of God; yonder Sinai quaked
at the presence of God, the God of Israel.
[9] You, O God, did send a plentiful rain; You did
restore and confirm Your heritage when it
languished and was weary.
[10] Your flock found a dwelling place in it; You, O
God, in Your goodness did provide for the
poor and needy.

Psalm 73:1-12 (AMP)
Book Three
Psalm 73
A Psalm of Asaph.
[1] Truly God is [only] good to Israel, even to those
who are upright and pure in heart.
[2] But as for me, my feet were almost gone, my steps
had well-nigh slipped.
[3] For I was envious of the foolish and arrogant when
I saw the prosperity of the wicked.
[4] For they suffer no violent pangs in their death, but
their strength is firm.
[5] They are not in trouble as other men; neither are
they smitten and plagued like other men.
[6] Therefore pride is about their necks like a chain;
violence covers them like a garment [like a long,
luxurious robe].
[7] Their eyes stand out with fatness, they have more

than heart could wish; and the imaginations of their
minds overflow [with follies].
[8] They scoff, and wickedly utter oppression; they
speak loftily [from on high, maliciously and
blasphemously].
[9] They set their mouths against and speak down
from heaven, and their tongues swagger through the
earth [invading even heaven with blasphemy and
smearing earth with slanders].
[10] Therefore His people return here, and waters of a
full cup [offered by the wicked] are [blindly]
drained by them.
[11] And they say, How does God know? Is there
knowledge in the Most High?
[12] Behold, these are the ungodly, who always
prosper and are at ease in the world; they increase in
riches.

Psalm 82 (NASB)
Unjust Judgments Rebuked.
A Psalm of Asaph.
[1] God takes His stand in His own congregation;
He judges in the midst of the rulers.
[2] How long will you judge unjustly
And show partiality to the wicked? Selah.
[3] Vindicate the weak and fatherless;
Do justice to the afflicted and destitute.
[4] Rescue the weak and needy;
Deliver them out of the hand of the wicked.
[5] They do not know nor do they understand;
They walk about in darkness;

All the foundations of the earth are shaken.

⁶ I said, "You are gods,

And all of you are sons of the Most High.

⁷ "Nevertheless you will die like men

And fall like any one of the princes."

⁸ Arise, O God, judge the earth!

For it is You who possesses all the nations.

Who are the wicked? The wicked are those who are in opposition to helping the weak, fatherless, afflicted, destitute and needy.

Psalm 94 (AMP)

¹ O Lord God, You to Whom vengeance belongs, O God, You to Whom vengeance belongs, shine forth!

² Rise up, O Judge of the earth; render to the proud a fit compensation!

³ Lord, how long shall the wicked, how long shall the wicked triumph and exult?

⁴ They pour out arrogant words, speaking hard things; all the evildoers boast loftily.

⁵ They crush Your people, O Lord, and afflict Your heritage.

⁶ They slay the widow and the transient stranger and murder the unprotected orphan.

⁷ Yet they say, The Lord does not see, neither does the God of Jacob notice it.

⁸ Consider and understand, you stupid ones among the people! And you [self-confident] fools, when will you become wise?

⁹ He Who planted the ear, shall He not hear? He Who formed the eye, shall He not see?

[10] He Who disciplines and instructs the nations, shall He not punish, He Who teaches man knowledge?
[11] The Lord knows the thoughts of man, that they are vain (empty and futile—only a breath).
[12] Blessed (happy, fortunate, to be envied) is the man whom You discipline and instruct, O Lord, and teach out of Your law,
[13] That You may give him power to keep himself calm in the days of adversity, until the [inevitable] pit of corruption is dug for the wicked.
[14] For the Lord will not cast off nor spurn His people, neither will He abandon His heritage.
[15] For justice will return to the [uncompromisingly] righteous, and all the upright in heart will follow it.
[16] Who will rise up for me against the evildoers? Who will stand up for me against the workers of iniquity?
[17] Unless the Lord had been my help, I would soon have dwelt in [the land where there is] silence.
[18] When I said, My foot is slipping, Your mercy and loving-kindness, O Lord, held me up.
[19] In the multitude of my [anxious] thoughts within me, Your comforts cheer and delight my soul!
[20] Shall the throne of iniquity have fellowship with You—they who frame and hide their unrighteous doings under [the sacred name of] law?
[21] They band themselves together against the life of the [consistently] righteous and condemn the innocent to death.
[22] But the Lord has become my High Tower and Defense, and my God the Rock of my refuge.

²³ And He will turn back upon them their own
iniquity and will wipe them out by means of their
own wickedness; the Lord our God will wipe them
out.

Who is it that takes away from the people the things that help them? The bible calls these oppressors of the people wicked. Are you voting for them? Are you absolutely positive that you're not?

Psalm 102:16-17 (NASB)
¹⁶ For the Lord has built up Zion;
He has appeared in His glory.
¹⁷ He has regarded the prayer of the destitute
And has not despised their prayer.

Psalm 106:1-3 (NASB)
Israel's Rebelliousness and
the Lord's Deliverances.
¹ Praise the Lord!
Oh give thanks to the Lord, for He is good;
For His lovingkindness is everlasting.
² Who can speak of the mighty deeds of the Lord,
Or can show forth all His praise?
³ How blessed are those who keep justice,
Who practice righteousness at all times!

Psalm 107:41-43 (NASB)
⁴¹ But He sets the needy securely on high away from
affliction,
And makes his families like a flock.
⁴² The upright see it and are glad;

But all unrighteousness shuts its mouth.
[43] Who is wise? Let him give heed to these things,
And consider the lovingkindnesses of the Lord.

As we can see in verse 41, God sets the needy securely on high away from affliction. According to verse 42, the political parties that would try to do this by helping the needy are known biblically as the upright. According to this psalm, the unrighteous appear to be angry about helping the needy. Are you voting unrighteously by voting against helping the needs of many?

Psalm 109:15-16 (NASB)

[15] Let them be before the Lord continually,
That He may cut off their memory from the earth;
[16] Because he did not remember to show lovingkindness,
But persecuted the afflicted and needy man,
And the despondent in heart, to put them to death.

In the end when Jesus returns, I would not want to be in the shoes of the politicians who worked against the needs of the people. And all just to be wealthy in this short lifetime. How short is this life in comparison to the eternity which we prepare, by our decisions in this short life.

Psalm 112 (AMP)

[1] Praise the Lord! (Hallelujah!) Blessed (happy, fortunate, to be envied) is the man who fears (reveres and worships) the Lord, who delights greatly in His commandments.
[2] His [spiritual] offspring shall be mighty upon earth; the generation of the upright shall be blessed.
[3] Prosperity and welfare are in his house, and his

righteousness endures forever.

⁴ Light arises in the darkness for the upright, gracious, compassionate, and just [who are in right standing with God].

⁵ It is well with the man who deals generously and lends, who conducts his affairs with justice.

⁶ He will not be moved forever; the [uncompromisingly] righteous (the upright, in right standing with God) shall be in everlasting remembrance.

⁷ IIc shall nut be afraid of evil tidings; his heart is firmly fixed, trusting (leaning on and being confident) in the Lord.

⁸ His heart is established and steady, he will not be afraid while he waits to see his desire established upon his adversaries.

⁹ He has distributed freely [he has given to the poor and needy]; his righteousness (uprightness and right standing with God) endures forever; his horn shall be exalted in honor.

¹⁰ The wicked man will see it and be grieved and angered, he will gnash his teeth and disappear [in despair]; the desire of the wicked shall perish and come to nothing.

Psalm 113:5-8 (NASB)

⁵ Who is like the Lord our God,
Who is enthroned on high,

⁶ Who humbles Himself to behold
The things that are in heaven and in the earth?

⁷ He raises the poor from the dust

And lifts the needy from the ash heap,
[8] To make them sit with princes,
With the princes of His people.

Psalm 125 (NASB)
The Lord Surrounds His People.
A Song of Ascents.

[1] Those who trust in the Lord
Are as Mount Zion, which cannot be moved
but abides forever.
[2] As the mountains surround Jerusalem,
So the Lord surrounds His people
From this time forth and forever.
[3] For the scepter of wickedness shall not rest upon
the land of the righteous,
So that the righteous will not put forth their hands to
do wrong.
[4] Do good, O Lord, to those who are good
And to those who are upright in their hearts.
[5] But as for those who turn aside to their crooked
ways,
The Lord will lead them away with the doers of
iniquity.
Peace be upon Israel.

Psalm 138:6 (NASB)

[6] For though the Lord is exalted,
Yet He regards the lowly,
But the haughty He knows from afar.

Psalm 140:1-2 (NASB)
Prayer for Protection against the Wicked.
For the choir director. A Psalm of David.
¹ Rescue me, O Lord, from evil men;
Preserve me from violent men
² Who devise evil things in their hearts;
They continually stir up wars.

Why do the same politicians that always want to take away from the people, by cutting Social Security, Medicare, Medicaid, and many other extremely important parts of government, why do these politicians who are against these good important things, why do they never seem to question the cost of more defense spending for more wars? Why? Is it because there is so much money in war spending for them, that no one ever questions? They will be ridiculously wealthy in this lifetime, but I surely don't envy their future. If they ask God to change them and save them from their destructive ways, I believe it's not too late for them if they are serious about changing. Surely God knows if they are serious or not.

Psalm 140:12-13 (NASB)
¹² I know that the Lord will maintain the cause of
the afflicted
And justice for the poor.
¹³ Surely the righteous will give thanks to Your
name;
The upright will dwell in Your presence.

Psalm 147:5-6 (NASB)
⁵ Great is our Lord and abundant in strength;
His understanding is infinite.

[6] The Lord supports the afflicted;
He brings down the wicked to the ground.

Proverbs 3:27-29 (NASB)

[27] Do not withhold good from those to whom it is
due,
When it is in your power to do it.
[28] Do not say to your neighbor, "Go, and come back,
And tomorrow I will give it,"
When you have it with you.
[29] Do not devise harm against your neighbor,
While he lives securely beside you.

Hello congress people are you listening? Voters?

Proverbs 3:33-35 (NASB)

[33] The curse of the Lord is on the house of the
wicked,
But He blesses the dwelling of the righteous.
[34] Though He scoffs at the scoffers,
Yet He gives grace to the afflicted.
[35] The wise will inherit honor,
But fools display dishonor.

Proverbs 10:2 (NASB)

[2] Ill-gotten gains do not profit,
But righteousness delivers from death.

Proverbs 11:4-6
New American Standard Bible (NASB)

[4] Riches do not profit in the day of wrath,

But righteousness delivers from death.
[5] The righteousness of the blameless will smooth his way,
But the wicked will fall by his own wickedness.
[6] The righteousness of the upright will deliver them,
But the treacherous will be caught by their
own greed.

Proverbs 11:17 (NASB)
[17] The merciful man does himself good,
But the cruel man does himself harm.

Proverbs 16:8 (NASB)
[8] Better is a little with righteousness
Than great income with injustice.

Proverbs 16:19-20 (NASB)
[19] It is better to be humble in spirit with the lowly
Than to divide the spoil with the proud.
[20] He who gives attention to the word will find good,
And blessed is he who trusts in the Lord.

Proverbs 17:5 (NASB)
[5] He who mocks the poor taunts his Maker;
He who rejoices at calamity will not go unpunished.

Proverbs 17:15-16 (NKJV)
[15] He who justifies the wicked, and he who condemns the just,
Both of them alike are an abomination to the Lord.

[16] Why is there in the hand of a fool the purchase
price of wisdom,
Since he has no heart for it?

Proverbs 21:7-8 (NASB)

[7] The violence of the wicked will drag them away,
Because they refuse to act with justice.
[8] The way of a guilty man is crooked,
But as for the pure, his conduct is upright.

Proverbs 22:16 (NASB)

[16] He who oppresses the poor to make more for
himself
Or who gives to the rich, will only come to poverty.

Which political party in your nation cuts services that helped everyone, only to give more in tax breaks to the wealthiest people?

Proverbs 25:26 (GW)

[26] Like a muddied spring and a polluted well,
so is a righteous person who gives in to a wicked
person.

Proverbs 28:5-6 (NASB)

[5] Evil men do not understand justice,
But those who seek the Lord understand all things.
[6] Better is the poor who walks in his integrity
Than he who is crooked though he be rich.

Proverbs 28:10-11 (NASB)

[10] He who leads the upright astray in an evil way

Will himself fall into his own pit,
But the blameless will inherit good.
[11] The rich man is wise in his own eyes,
But the poor who has understanding sees through
him.

Proverbs 28:15-16 (NKJV)

[15] Like a roaring lion and a charging bear
Is a wicked ruler over poor people.
[16] A ruler who lacks understanding is a great
oppressor,
But he who hates covetousness will
prolong his days.

Most of the people in America who understand how expensive medicine has become, would agree that in their eyes, the wicked rulers are those who are against free, or very inexpensive healthcare for all. These are the oppressive leaders of a nation, the same ones who continually want more defense spending for more wars.

Proverbs 28:20-22 (NKJV)

[20] A faithful man will abound with blessings,
But he who hastens to be rich will not go
unpunished.
[21] To show partiality is not good,
Because for a piece of bread a man will transgress.
[22] A man with an evil eye hastens after riches,
And does not consider that poverty will come upon
him

Proverbs 29:2 (NASB)

[2] When the righteous increase, the people rejoice,
But when a wicked man rules, people groan.

Proverbs 29:4 (NASB)

[4] The king gives stability to the land by justice,
But a man who takes bribes overthrows it.

Proverbs 29:7 (NASB)

[7] The righteous is concerned for the rights of the poor,
The wicked does not understand such concern.

Proverbs 29:10 (NASB)

[10] Men of bloodshed hate the blameless,
But the upright are concerned for his life.

Proverbs 29:13-14 (NASB)

[13] The poor man and the oppressor have this in common:
The Lord gives light to the eyes of both.
[14] If a king judges the poor with truth,
His throne will be established forever.

Proverbs 30:12-14 (AMP)

[12] There is a class of people who are pure in their own eyes, and yet are not washed from their own filth.
[13] There is a class of people—oh, how lofty are their eyes and their raised eyelids!
[14] There is a class of people whose teeth are as

swords and whose fangs as knives, to devour the poor from the earth and the needy from among men.

Proverbs 31:4-5 (AMP)

[4] It is not for kings, O Lemuel, it is not for kings to drink wine, or for rulers to desire strong drink, [5] Lest they drink and forget the law and what it decrees, and pervert the justice due any of the afflicted.

Ecclesiastes 4:1-3 (NASB)
The Evils of Oppression

[1] Then I looked again at all the acts of oppression which were being done under the sun. And behold I saw the tears of the oppressed and that they had no one to comfort them; and on the side of their oppressors was power, but they had no one to comfort them. [2] So I congratulated the dead who are already dead more than the living who are still living. [3] But better off than both of them is the one who has never existed, who has never seen the evil activity that is done under the sun.

Ecclesiastes 5:8-10 (NASB)

[8] If you see oppression of the poor and denial of justice and righteousness in the province, do not be shocked at the sight; for one official watches over another official, and there are higher officials over them. [9] After all, a king who cultivates the field is an advantage to the land.

[10] He who loves money will not be satisfied with
money, nor he who loves abundance with
its income. This too is vanity.

Ecclesiastes 7:4 (NASB)

[4] The mind of the wise is in the house of mourning,
While the mind of fools is in the house of pleasure.

Ecclesiastes 7:7 (NASB)

[7] For oppression makes a wise man mad,
And a bribe corrupts the heart.

Isaiah 1:21-28 (NASB)
Zion Corrupted, to Be Redeemed

[21] How the faithful city has become a harlot,
She who was full of justice!
Righteousness once lodged in her,
But now murderers.
[22] Your silver has become dross,
Your drink diluted with water.
[23] Your rulers are rebels
And companions of thieves;
Everyone loves a bribe
And chases after rewards.
They do not defend the orphan,
Nor does the widow's plea come before them.
[24] Therefore the Lord God of hosts,
The Mighty One of Israel, declares,
"Ah, I will be relieved of My adversaries
And avenge Myself on My foes.
[25] "I will also turn My hand against you,

And will smelt away your dross as with lye
And will remove all your alloy.
²⁶ "Then I will restore your judges as at the first,
And your counselors as at the beginning;
After that you will be called the city of
righteousness,
A faithful city."
²⁷ Zion will be redeemed with justice
And her repentant ones with righteousness.
²⁸ But transgressors and sinners will be crushed
together,
And those who forsake the Lord will come to an
end.

Please Come Lord Jesus and deliver us all from the wicked who oppress the poor. And please open the eyes of those in your church to quit voting for them.

Isaiah 5:20-24 (NASB)
²⁰ Woe to those who call evil good, and good evil;
Who substitute darkness for light and light for
darkness;
Who substitute bitter for sweet and sweet for bitter!
²¹ Woe to those who are wise in their own eyes
And clever in their own sight!
²² Woe to those who are heroes in drinking wine
And valiant men in mixing strong drink,
²³ Who justify the wicked for a bribe,
And take away the rights of the ones who are in the
right!
²⁴ Therefore, as a tongue of fire consumes stubble

And dry grass collapses into the flame,
So their root will become like rot and their
blossom blow away as dust;
For they have rejected the law of the Lord of hosts
And despised the word of the Holy One of Israel.

Isaiah 10:1-3 (NASB)
Assyria Is God's Instrument

[1] Woe to those who enact evil statutes
And to those who constantly record unjust
decisions,
[2] So as to deprive the needy of justice
And rob the poor of My people of their rights,
So that widows may be their spoil
And that they may plunder the orphans.
[3] Now what will you do in the day of punishment,
And in the devastation which will come from afar?
To whom will you flee for help?
And where will you leave your wealth?

Isaiah 13:11 (NASB)

[11] Thus I will punish the world for its evil
And the wicked for their iniquity;
I will also put an end to the arrogance of the proud
And abase the haughtiness of the ruthless.

Isaiah 25:4-5 (NASB)

[4] For You have been a defense for the helpless,
A defense for the needy in his distress,
A refuge from the storm, a shade from the heat;
For the breath of the ruthless

Is like a rain storm against a wall.
[5] Like heat in drought, You subdue the uproar of
aliens;
Like heat by the shadow of a cloud, the song of the
ruthless is silenced.

Isaiah 26:4-6 (NASB)

[4] "Trust in the Lord forever,
For in God the Lord, we have an everlasting Rock.
[5] "For He has brought low those who dwell on high,
the unassailable city;
He lays it low, He lays it low to the ground, He
casts it to the dust.
[6] "The foot will trample it,
The feet of the afflicted, the steps of the helpless."

Jeremiah 20:11-13 (NASB)

[11] But the Lord is with me like a dread champion;
Therefore my persecutors will stumble and not
prevail.
They will be utterly ashamed, because they
have failed,
With an everlasting disgrace that will not be
forgotten.
[12] Yet, O Lord of hosts, You who test the righteous,
Who see the mind and the heart;
Let me see Your vengeance on them;
For to You I have set forth my cause.
[13] Sing to the Lord, praise the Lord!
For He has delivered the soul of the needy one
From the hand of evildoers.

Jeremiah 22:13-17 (NASB)

Messages about the Kings

[13] "Woe to him who builds his house without righteousness

And his upper rooms without justice,

Who uses his neighbor's services without pay

And does not give him his wages,

[14] Who says, 'I will build myself a roomy house

With spacious upper rooms,

And cut out its windows,

Paneling it with cedar and painting it bright red.'

[15] "Do you become a king because you are competing in cedar?

Did not your father eat and drink

And do justice and righteousness?

Then it was well with him.

[16] "He pled the cause of the afflicted and needy;

Then it was well.

Is not that what it means to know Me?"

Declares the Lord.

[17] "But your eyes and your heart

Are intent only upon your own dishonest gain,

And on shedding innocent blood

And on practicing oppression and extortion."

Church, please notice verse 16. Pleading the cause of the afflicted and needy is what it means to know the Lord. Could this be even more important to God then other things that we think are most important?

Ezekiel 16:48-50 (NASB)

[48] As I live," declares the Lord God, "Sodom, your

sister and her daughters have not done as you and your daughters have done. ⁴⁹ Behold, this was the guilt of your sister Sodom: she and her daughters had arrogance, abundant food and careless ease, but she did not help the poor and needy. ⁵⁰ Thus they were haughty and committed abominations before Me. Therefore I removed them when I saw it.

Ezekiel 22 (AMP)

¹ Moreover, the word of the Lord came to me, saying,

² And you son of man [Ezekiel], will you judge, will you judge the bloodshedding city? Then cause her to know all her abominations,

³ And say, Thus says the Lord God: A city that sheds blood in the midst of her so that her time [of doom] will come, and makes idols [over those who worship them] to defile her!

⁴ In your blood which you have shed you have become guilty, and you are defiled by the idols which you have made, and you have caused your time [of judgment and punishment] to draw near and have arrived at the full measure of your years. Therefore have I made you a reproach to the [heathen] nations and a mocking to all countries.

⁵ Those who are near and those who are far from you will mock you, you infamous one, full of tumult.

⁶ Behold, the princes of Israel in you, every one according to his power, have been intending to shed blood.

[7] In you have they treated father and mother lightly; in the midst of you they have dealt unjustly and by oppression in relation to the stranger; in you they have wronged the fatherless and the widow.

[8] You have despised and scorned My sacred things and have profaned My Sabbaths.

[9] In you are slanderous men who arouse suspicions to shed blood, and in you are they who have eaten [food offered to idols] upon the mountains; in the midst of you they have committed lewdness.

[10] In you men have uncovered their fathers' nakedness [the nakedness of mother or stepmother]; in you they have humbled women who are [ceremonially] unclean [during their periods or because of childbirth].

[11] And one has committed abomination with his neighbor's wife, another has lewdly defiled his daughter-in-law, and another in you has humbled his sister, his father's daughter.

[12] In you they have accepted bribes to shed blood; you have taken [forbidden] interest and [percentage of] increase, and you have greedily gained from your neighbors by oppression and extortion and have forgotten Me, says the Lord God.

[13] Behold therefore, I have struck My hands together at your dishonest gain which you have made and at the blood which has been in the midst of you.

[14] Can your heart and courage endure or can your hands be strong in the days that I shall deal with you? I the Lord have spoken it, and I will do it.

[15] And I will scatter you among the nations and

disperse you through the countries, and I will consume your filthiness out of you.

¹⁶ And you shall be dishonored and profane yourself in the sight of the nations, and you shall know (understand and realize) that I am the Lord.

¹⁷ And the word of the Lord came to me, saying,

¹⁸ Son of man, the house of Israel has become to Me scum and waste matter. All of them are bronze and tin and iron and lead in the midst of the furnace; they are the dross of silver.

¹⁹ Therefore thus says the Lord God: Because you have all become scum and waste matter, behold therefore, I will gather you [O Israel] into the midst of Jerusalem.

²⁰ As they gather silver and bronze and iron and lead and tin into the midst of the furnace, to blow the fire upon it in order to melt it, so will I gather you in My anger and in My wrath, and I will put you in and melt you.

²¹ Yes, I will gather you and blow upon you with the fire of My wrath, and you shall be melted in the midst of it.

²² As silver is melted in the midst of the furnace, so shall you be melted in the midst of it, and you shall know, understand, and realize that I the Lord have poured out My wrath upon you [O Israel].

²³ And the word of the Lord came to me, saying,

²⁴ Son of man, say to her, You are a land that is not cleansed nor rained upon in the day of indignation.

²⁵ There is a conspiracy of [Israel's false] prophets in the midst of her, like a roaring lion tearing the

prey; they have devoured human lives; they have taken [in their greed] treasure and precious things; they have made many widows in the midst of her.
[26] Her priests have done violence to My law and have profaned My holy things. They have made no distinction between the sacred and the secular, neither have they taught people the difference between the unclean and the clean and have hid their eyes from My Sabbaths, and I am profaned among them.
[27] Her princes in the midst of her are like wolves rending and devouring the prey, shedding blood and destroying lives to get dishonest gain.
[28] And her prophets have daubed them over with whitewash, seeing false visions and divining lies to them, saying, Thus says the Lord God—when the Lord has not spoken.
[29] The people of the land have used oppression and extortion and have committed robbery; yes, they have wronged and vexed the poor and needy; yes, they have oppressed the stranger and temporary resident wrongfully.
[30] And I sought a man among them who should build up the wall and stand in the gap before Me for the land, that I should not destroy it, but I found none.
[31] Therefore have I poured out My indignation upon them; I have consumed them with the fire of My wrath; their own way have I repaid [by bringing it] upon their own heads, says the Lord God.

Daniel 4:27 (NASB)

27 Therefore, O king, may my advice be pleasing to you: break away now from your sins
by doing righteousness and from your iniquities
by showing mercy to the poor, in case there may be
a prolonging of your prosperity.'

Amos 2:6-7 (NASB)

6 Thus says the Lord,
"For three transgressions of Israel and for four
I will not revoke its punishment,
Because they sell the righteous for money
And the needy for a pair of sandals.
7 "These who pant after the very dust of the earth on the head of the helpless
Also turn aside the way of the humble;
And a man and his father resort to the same girl
In order to profane My holy name.

Amos 4:1-2 (NASB)
"Yet You Have Not Returned to Me"

1 Hear this word, you cows of Bashan who are on the mountain of Samaria,
Who oppress the poor, who crush the needy,
Who say to your husbands, "Bring now, that we may drink!"
2 The Lord God has sworn by His holiness,
"Behold, the days are coming upon you
When they will take you away with meat hooks,
And the last of you with fish hooks.

Amos 5:6-15 (NASB)

[6] "Seek the Lord that you may live,

Or He will break forth like a fire, O house of

Joseph,

And it will consume with none to quench it for

Bethel,

[7] For those who turn justice into wormwood

And cast righteousness down to the earth."

[8] He who made the Pleiades and Orion

And changes deep darkness into morning,

Who also darkens day into night,

Who calls for the waters of the sea

And pours them out on the surface of the earth,

The Lord is His name.

[9] It is He who flashes forth with destruction upon

the strong,

So that destruction comes upon the fortress.

[10] They hate him who reproves in the gate,

And they abhor him who speaks with integrity.

[11] Therefore because you impose heavy rent on the

poor

And exact a tribute of grain from them,

Though you have built houses of well-hewn stone,

Yet you will not live in them;

You have planted pleasant vineyards, yet you

will not drink their wine.

[12] For I know your transgressions are many and your

sins are great,

You who distress the righteous and accept bribes

And turn aside the poor in the gate.

[13] Therefore at such a time the prudent person keeps

silent, for it is an evil time.

[14] Seek good and not evil, that you may live;

And thus may the Lord God of hosts be with you,

Just as you have said!

[15] Hate evil, love good,

And establish justice in the gate!

Perhaps the Lord God of hosts

May be gracious to the remnant of Joseph.

Obadiah 1:15 (NASB)
The Day of the Lord and the Future

[15] "For the day of the Lord draws near on all the nations.

As you have done, it will be done to you.

Your dealings will return on your own head.

As you have done, it will be done to you. Your dealings will return on your own head. Any questions politicians?

Zechariah 1:3-6 (NASB)

[3] Therefore say to them, 'Thus says the Lord of hosts, "Return to Me," declares the Lord of hosts, "that I may return to you," says the Lord of hosts. [4] "Do not be like your fathers, to whom the former prophets proclaimed, saying, 'Thus says the Lord of hosts, "Return now from your evil ways and from your evil deeds."' But they did not listen or give heed to Me," declares the Lord. [5] "Your fathers, where are they? And the prophets, do they live forever? [6] But did not My words and My statutes, which I commanded My

servants the prophets, overtake your fathers? Then they repented and said, 'As the Lord of hosts purposed to do to us in accordance with our ways and our deeds, so He has dealt with us.'""

1 Timothy 6:17-19 (NASB)

[17] Instruct those who are rich in this present world not to be conceited or to fix their hope on the uncertainty of riches, but on God, who richly supplies us with all things to enjoy. [18] Instruct them to do good, to be rich in good works, to be generous and ready to share, [19] storing up for themselves the treasure of a good foundation for the future, so that they may take hold of that which is life indeed."

James 2:12-13 (NASB)

[12] So speak and act as those who are to be judged by the law of liberty. [13] For judgment will be merciless to one who has shown no mercy; mercy triumphs over judgment.

James 5:1-6 (NASB)
Misuse of Riches

[1] Come now, you rich, weep and howl for your miseries which are coming upon you. [2] Your riches have rotted and your garments have become moth-eaten. [3] Your gold and your silver have rusted; and their rust will be a witness against you and will consume your flesh like fire. It is in the last days that you have stored up your treasure! [4] Behold, the

pay of the laborers who mowed your
fields, and which has been withheld by you, cries
out against you; and the outcry of those who did the
harvesting has reached the ears of the Lord
of Sabaoth. [5] You have lived luxuriously on the
earth and led a life of wanton pleasure; you
have fattened your hearts in a day of
slaughter. [6] You have condemned and put to
death the righteous man; he does not resist you.

And so shall it be that the oppressed will have great victory over the oppressors in the end.

CHAPTER NINE
Thoughts of the Kingdom of God and of His Character

For a fool speaks nonsense, and his heart inclines toward wickedness, to practice ungodliness and to speak error against the Lord, to keep the hungry person unsatisfied, and to withhold drink from the thirsty. As for a rogue, his weapons are evil, he devises wicked schemes to destroy the afflicted with slander, even though the needy one speaks what is right. These are not my words, you will see them later in this chapter from Isaiah chapter 32. Take another good look at these words you professed Christian politicians and Christian voters. How does your political party of choice line up to these words in their political desires of law making? If you are a Christian politician, should you really want to be on the side of the oppressors like this wicked, ungodly, evil destroying person above, who speaks in error against the Lord? And if you're a Christian voter, should you want to vote for people like this? What are the bible politics of this scripture? Which political parties most resemble it? It would be the political parties that work against the poor, afflicted and needy in cutting government services that help to eliminate needs for the majority of the people. Do you think heaven will be the end of government? Does God give us any idea about this? Yes He does as a matter of fact, in this next scripture.

Isaiah 9:6-7 (NASB)
[6] For a child will be born to us, a son will be given
to us;
And the government will rest on His shoulders;
And His name will be called Wonderful
Counselor, Mighty God,

Eternal Father, Prince of Peace.
[7] There will be no end to the increase
of His government or of peace,
On the throne of David and over his kingdom,
To establish it and to uphold it with justice and
righteousness
From then on and forevermore.
The zeal of the Lord of hosts will accomplish this.

Yes there will be government in heaven, sorry to be the bearer of bad news to you haters of government. The government will rest on the shoulders of one whose name is Wonderful Councilor, Mighty God, Eternal Father, Prince of Peace. Do you believe the Prince of Peace would want the healthcare needs of all taken care of, as reasonably as possible (maybe even free) through His government, which would be an increase to the size of government, or do you believe that He would be against the increase in size of government like our politicians who oppose much more affordable government healthcare for all, which would be a shrinking or downsizing of our government? Would the Prince of Peace cut social security and hurt the vast majority of the people in order to shrink government, or would He want to strengthen Social Security for the sake of helping the vast majority of the people which would essentially be an increase of government?

Please look at verse 7 again which says "there will be no end to the increase of His government or of peace." Who is more at peace, sick people whose expenses of sickness are covered by their government or sick people who have to sell their home just because they got sick? God's government will be upheld with justice and righteousness as you have just read, and would never allow for such misery to happen to anyone. I have heard pastors and others that work in ministry who speak as though they don't like government very much. I sure hope for their sake that they are not too disappointed with heaven's ever increasing government.

Isaiah 11:1-5 (NASB)

Righteous Reign of the Branch

[1] Then a shoot will spring from the stem of Jesse,

And a branch from his roots will bear fruit.

[2] The Spirit of the Lord will rest on Him,

The spirit of wisdom and understanding,

The spirit of counsel and strength,

The spirit of knowledge and the fear of the Lord.

[3] And He will delight in the fear of the Lord,

And He will not judge by what His eyes see,

Nor make a decision by what His ears hear;

[4] But with righteousness He will judge the poor,

And decide with fairness for the afflicted of the earth;

And He will strike the earth with the rod of His mouth,

And with the breath of His lips He will slay the wicked.

[5] Also righteousness will be the belt about His loins,

And faithfulness the belt about His waist.

Isaiah 14:30-32 (NASB)

[30] "Those who are most helpless will eat,

And the needy will lie down in security;

I will destroy your root with famine,

And it will kill off your survivors.

[31] "Wail, O gate; cry, O city;

Melt away, O Philistia, all of you;

For smoke comes from the north,

And there is no straggler in his ranks.

[32] "How then will one answer the messengers of the nation?

That the Lord has founded Zion,

And the afflicted of His people will seek refuge in it."

Isaiah 19:19-20 (NASB)

[19] In that day there will be an altar to the Lord in the midst of the land of Egypt, and a pillar to the Lord near its border. [20] It will become a sign and a witness to the Lord of hosts in the land of Egypt; for they will cry to the Lord because of oppressors, and He will send them a Savior and a Champion, and He will deliver them.

How incredibly short are everyone's lives here on Earth compared to our eternal destiny which awaits us all biblically. The oppressors are so wealthy and powerful in this world, but I surely do not envy their future. Will their wealth and worldly power take them down, or will they repent to God and change their ways?

Isaiah 16:3-5 (NASB)

[3] "Give us advice, make a decision;

Cast your shadow like night at high noon;

Hide the outcasts, do not betray the fugitive.

[4] "Let the outcasts of Moab stay with you;

Be a hiding place to them from the destroyer."

For the extortioner has come to an end, destruction has ceased,

Oppressors have completely disappeared from the land.

[5] A throne will even be established in lovingkindness,

And a judge will sit on it in faithfulness in the tent
of David;
Moreover, he will seek justice
And be prompt in righteousness.

Isaiah 32:1-7 (NASB)
The Glorious Future
[1] Behold, a king will reign righteously
And princes will rule justly.
[2] Each will be like a refuge from the wind
And a shelter from the storm,
Like streams of water in a dry country,
Like the shade of a huge rock in a parched land.
[3] Then the eyes of those who see will not be blinded,
And the ears of those who hear will listen.
[4] The mind of the hasty will discern the truth,
And the tongue of the stammerers will hasten to
speak clearly.
[5] No longer will the fool be called noble,
Or the rogue be spoken of as generous.
[6] For a fool speaks nonsense,
And his heart inclines toward wickedness:
To practice ungodliness and to speak error against
the Lord,
To keep the hungry person unsatisfied
And to withhold drink from the thirsty.
[7] As for a rogue, his weapons are evil;
He devises wicked schemes
To destroy the afflicted with slander,
Even though the needy one speaks what is right.

Isaiah 54:11-15 (NASB)

[11] "O afflicted one, storm-tossed, and not comforted,

Behold, I will set your stones in antimony,

And your foundations I will lay in sapphires.

[12] "Moreover, I will make your battlements

of rubies,

And your gates of crystal,

And your entire wall of precious stones.

[13] "All your sons will be taught of the Lord;

And the well-being of your sons will be great.

[14] "In righteousness you will be established;

You will be far from oppression, for you will not

fear;

And from terror, for it will not come near you.

[15] "If anyone fiercely assails you it will not be from

Me.

Whoever assails you will fall because of you.

Just another example that oppression is not from God, God is way beyond generous, and His children should also be generous.

Isaiah 55:1-2 (NASB)
The Free Offer of Mercy

[1] "Ho! Every one who thirsts, come to the waters;

And you who have no money come, buy and eat.

Come, buy wine and milk

Without money and without cost.

[2] "Why do you spend money for what is not bread,

And your wages for what does not satisfy?

Listen carefully to Me, and eat what is good,

And delight yourself in abundance.

Jeremiah 9:23-24 (NASB)

[23] Thus says the Lord, "Let not a wise man boast of his wisdom, and let not the mighty man boast of his might, let not a rich man boast of his riches; [24] but let him who boasts boast of this, that he understands and knows Me, that I am the Lord who exercises lovingkindness, justice and righteousness on earth; for I delight in these things," declares the Lord.

Let's take another look at America's 2 major political parties the Democrats and the Republicans side by side. Which do you believe is more in line with true biblical Christianity in eliminating the needs of all people, and which party is more in line biblically to being the oppressor?

The (More Liberal) Democrat Way of Governing the People's Money.

Tax the wealthiest 1% of Americans adequately enough

AND

Spend less on defense for war

In order for America to provide its people:

• Very affordable healthcare for all people, keep Medicare and Medicaid strong.

• Keep Social Security strong, keep retirement age 62.

• Well-funded quality public schools, quality teachers, books, sports

• Well-funded city bus lines, subways, inexpensive public transportation for all.

• Well-funded city parks and public libraries.

• Well-funded street, highway, and bridge repair to keep roads smooth and safe.

• Well-funded public utility works, lights, water, sewer, snow removal, grass cutting, etc.

• Well-funded police and fire protection for all.

• Well-funded continued research in alternative clean energy sources such as solar, wind & others such as electric vehicles to create jobs and become less reliant on fossil fuels.

• Well-funded E.P.A. Environmental Protection Agency to help ensure clean air and water for all through government regulation of corporate polluters, to keep them honest and to keep pollution to the lowest levels possible.

• Well-funded food inspection.

• Well-funded assistance for food stamps and heat assistance for the poor, many who work.

The Conservative Republican Way of Governing the People's Money.

Reduce taxes on the wealthiest 1% as much as possible

AND

Spend more on defense for war

By cutting funding to government services for the people such as:

• Cut Medicare and Medicaid

• Cut Social Security and raise the retirement age

• Cut public education, schools, teachers, books, sports

• Cut funding to bus lines and affordable public transportation

• Cut funding to city parks and public libraries

• Cut street, highway and bridge repair

• Cut public utility works

• Cut police officers and firefighters

• Cut research in alternative clean energy sources such as solar, wind, and electric vehicles

• Cut E.P.A. Environmental Protection Agency and deregulate corporations to freely pollute the air and water keeping pollution on the rise, making some water undrinkable and air dangerous to breath.

• Cut food inspection

• Cut assistance for food stamps and heat assistance for the poor, many of whom work.

Other Differences About Democrats

(No corporate (for profit) control of government)

• Keep police and firefighters government controlled and not owned and operated by for profit corporations.

• Keep prisons government operated and not owned and operated by for profit corporations.

• Keep our 238 year old postal system government operated and not owned and operated by for profit corporations because it's never taken any tax dollars to operate.

• Keep government regulation of banks for the protection of the people to keep banks accountable and honest, also keeping the FDIC to ensure most peoples' savings in banks are safe.

• Keep sex education and abstinence training and regulate insurers to provide contraception to attempt to keep abortions and unwanted pregnancies to a minimum.

• Let immigrants become citizens, work, and pay tax to help the economy.

• Keep unions strong to give working people the strong voice of collective bargaining against corporate greed.

• In favor of the National Labor Relations Board for the American worker to have rights.

• Keep jobs in America instead of shipping them overseas.

• Strengthen the Voting Rights Act of 1965 to keep voting rights for all people fair, easy and strong. No difficult forms of ID required. Keep accessible same day registration. Make voting faster and easier to keep length of voting lines as short as possible.

• Democrats are very much against the sequester cuts which are not necessary and do nothing but hurt many people along with hurting America's economy.

Other Differences About Republicans

(Allow private corporations to take control of government services for profit)

• Allow private corporations to own and operate police officers and firefighters for profit.

• Allow private (for profit) corporations to own and operate prisons instead of government.

• Allow private corporations to take over America's successful 238 year old postal system for profit.

• Deregulate banks and enable them to be much less accountable for their actions.

• Cut sex education and contraception coverage.

• Spend billions of dollars keeping immigrants illegal and unable to pay tax into our government.

• Get rid of unions and the working people's voice to collectively bargain against corporate greed.

• Not in favor of the National Labor Relations Board for the American worker to have rights.

• In favor of shipping American jobs overseas.

• Weaken the Voting Rights Act of 1965 to make voting more difficult. Harder and more expensive forms of I.D. required. Some ending of accessible same day registration. Longer voting lines are inevitable with the Republican voter ID laws.

• Republicans are in favor of the sequester cuts.

CHAPTER TEN
Attempting To Biblically Define the Words
Liberal and Conservative

We have liberal and conservative political parties across the world. The words liberal and conservative are commonly misrepresented by many. If we consider ourselves Christians, wouldn't it make sense for us to find the biblical definitions of these 2 words, that we may not misrepresent them? I have searched 44 English versions of the bible for the words liberal and conservative. 30 of the 44 versions had either the word liberal and/or variations of it, such as liberally and liberality. 2 of the 44 versions had the word conservative. First we will look at the 2 versions which have the word conservative, they are the Message bible and the Voice bible versions, together using the word conservative in a total of 3 examples, once in the Message, twice in the Voice. The word liberal and its variations can be found up to 11 times in the bible depending on which version you have. The Amplified bible version has all 11, so we will look only at the Amplified bible for the word liberal and its variations. Here first are the 3 examples with the word conservative.

Galatians 2:11-13 (MSG)
Later, when Peter came to Antioch, I had a face-to-face confrontation with him because he was clearly out of line. Here's the situation. Earlier, before certain persons had come from James, Peter regularly ate with the non-Jews. But when that **conservative** group came from Jerusalem, he cautiously pulled back and put as much distance as

he could manage between himself and his non-Jewish friends. That's how fearful he was of the **conservative** Jewish clique that's been pushing the old system of circumcision. Unfortunately, the rest of the Jews in the Antioch church joined in that hypocrisy so that even Barnabas was swept along in the charade.

Luke 20:21 (VOICE)

In addition to the Pharisees, there is a religious sect in Roman-occupied Israel called the Sadducees. They are religious **conservatives** holding to an ancient tradition in Judaism that doesn't believe in an afterlife. Their disbelief in an afterlife seems to make them conclude, "There's only one life, and this is it, so you'd better play it safe." That means they are very happy to collaborate with the Romans—and make a healthy profit—rather than risk any kind of rebellion or revolt. For this reason, they are closely allied with another group called the Herodians, allies of Caesar's puppet king Herod. Their contemporaries, the Pharisees, who believe in an afterlife, are more prone to risk their lives in a rebellion since they hope martyrs will be rewarded with resurrection. For this reason, the Pharisees are closely allied with the Zealots, who are more overtly revolutionary. Each group tries to trap Jesus, but He turns the tables on them, using each encounter to shed more light on the message of the kingdom of God. In case after case, Jesus brings His hearers to the heart of the matter; and again and again, the bottom-line issue is money.

Chief Priests, Religious Scholars, and Elders:
Teacher, we respect You because You speak and
teach only what is right, You show no partiality to
anyone, and You truly teach the way of God.

Acts 23:6 (VOICE)
Paul is brilliant. Accused by a group of religious
intellectuals, he gets them fighting with one another.
Paul understands the axiom, "The enemy of my
enemy is my friend," so he picks a fight with the
Sadducees knowing the rest of the room will defend
him. The thing society opposes often defines it, so
manipulation is easy. (Consider some of the
conservative political pundits who have never
espoused any inclination toward Christianity. They
gain millions of Christian followers by opposing the
political enemies of **conservative** Christians.) Paul
embraces a similar strategy here—if he can get
these guys to fight, they will forget why they are
actually convening. In many ways, the culture war
is equally distracting to the early church. In the
middle of the Jews vs. Gentiles battle, the church is
realizing believers are not here to fight about
morality and culture, but to bring the kingdom of
God to earth. His kingdom will not come by debate,
but by the working of the Holy Spirit within the
church.
[6] Paul noticed that some members of the council
were Sadducees and some were Pharisees, so he
quickly spoke to the council.
Paul: Brothers, I am a Pharisee, born to a Pharisee.

I am on trial because I have hope that the dead are
raised!

Regarding the biblical definition of the word conservative, I believe there
may be some variance within groups of people as to the proper interpretation.
Therefore I will make no judgment as to the proper definition, but will leave it for
you to examine. Now here are the 11 biblical examples of the word liberal and its
variations.

Deuteronomy 15:1-14 (AMP)

[1] At the end of every seven years you shall grant a
release.

[2] And this is the manner of the release: every
creditor shall release that which he has lent to his
neighbor; he shall not exact it of his neighbor, his
brother, for the Lord's release is proclaimed.

[3] Of a foreigner you may exact it, but whatever of
yours is with your brother [Israelite] your hand
shall release.

[4] But there will be no poor among you, for the Lord
will surely bless you in the land which the Lord
your God gives you for an inheritance to possess,

[5] If only you carefully listen to the voice of the Lord
your God, to do watchfully all these
commandments which I command you this day.

[6] When the Lord your God blesses you as He
promised you, then you shall lend to many nations,
but you shall not borrow; and you shall rule over
many nations, but they shall not rule over you.

[7] If there is among you a poor man, one of your
kinsmen in any of the towns of your land which the

Lord your God gives you, you shall not harden your [minds and] hearts or close your hands to your poor brother;

[8] But you shall open your hands wide to him and shall surely lend him sufficient for his need in whatever he lacks.

[9] Beware lest there be a base thought in your [minds and] hearts, and you say, The seventh year, the year of release, is at hand, and your eye be evil against your poor brother and you give him nothing, and he cry to the Lord against you, and it be sin in you.

[10] You shall give to him freely without begrudging it; because of this the Lord will bless you in all your work and in all you undertake.

[11] For the poor will never cease out of the land; therefore I command you, You shall open wide your hands to your brother, to your needy, and to your poor in your land.

[12] And if your brother, a Hebrew man or a Hebrew woman, is sold to you and serves you six years, then in the seventh year you shall let him go free from you.

[13] And when you send him out free from you, you shall not let him go away empty-handed.

[14] You shall furnish him **liberally** out of your flock, your threshing floor, and your winepress; of what the Lord your God has blessed you, you shall give to him.

Esther 1:1-7 (AMP)

[1] It was in the days of Ahasuerus [Xerxes], the

Ahasuerus who reigned from India to Ethiopia over 127 provinces.

² In those days when King Ahasuerus sat on his royal throne which was in Shushan or Susa [the capital of the Persian Empire] in the palace or castle,

³ In the third year of his reign he made a feast for all his princes and his courtiers. The chief officers of the Persian and Median army and the nobles and governors of the provinces were there before him

⁴ While he showed the riches of his glorious kingdom and the splendor and excellence of his majesty for many days, even 180 days.

⁵ And when these days were completed, the king made a feast for all the people present in Shushan the capital, both great and small, a seven-day feast in the court of the garden of the king's palace.

⁶ There were hangings of fine white cloth, of green and of blue [cotton], fastened with cords of fine linen and purple to silver rings or rods and marble pillars. The couches of gold and silver rested on a [mosaic] pavement of porphyry, white marble, mother-of-pearl, and [precious] colored stones.

⁷ Drinks were served in different kinds of golden goblets, and there was royal wine in abundance, according to the **liberality** of the king.

Job 21:15-30 (AMP)

¹⁵ Who is the Almighty, that we should serve Him? And what profit do we have if we pray to Him?
¹⁶ But notice, [you say] the prosperity of the wicked

is not in their power; the mystery [of God's dealings] with the ungodly is far from my comprehension.

[17] How often [then] is it that the lamp of the wicked is put out? That their calamity comes upon them? That God distributes pains and sorrows to them in His anger?

[18] That they are like stubble before the wind and like chaff that the storm steals and carries away?

[19] You say, God lays up [the punishment of the wicked man's] iniquity for his children. Let Him recompense it to the man himself, that he may know and feel it.

[20] Let his own eyes see his destruction, and let him drink of the wrath of the Almighty.

[21] For what pleasure or interest has a man in his house and family after he is dead, when the number of his months is cut off?

[22] Shall any teach God knowledge, seeing that He judges those who are on high?

[23] One dies in his full strength, being wholly at ease and quiet;

[24] His pails are full of milk [his veins are filled with nourishment], and the marrow of his bones is fresh and moist,

[25] Whereas another man dies in bitterness of soul and never tastes of pleasure or good fortune.

[26] They lie down alike in the dust, and the worm spreads a covering over them.

[27] Behold, I know your thoughts and plans and the devices with which you would wrong me.

[28] For you say, Where is the house of the
rich and **liberal** prince [meaning me]? And where is
the tent in which the wicked [Job] dwelt?
[29] Have you not asked those who travel this way,
and do you not accept their
testimony and evidences—
[30] That the evil man is [now] spared in the day of
calamity and destruction, and they are led
forth and away on the day of [God's] wrath?

Proverbs 11:25 (AMP)

[25] The **liberal** person shall be enriched, and he who
waters shall himself be watered.

Proverbs 19:6 (AMP)

[6] Many will entreat the favor of a **liberal** man, and
every man is a friend to him who gives gifts.

Isaiah 32:8 (AMP)

[8] But the noble, openhearted, and **liberal** man
devises noble things; and he stands for what is
noble, openhearted, and generous.

Romans 12:8 (AMP)

[8] He who exhorts (encourages), to his exhortation;
he who contributes, let him do it in
simplicity and **liberality**; he who gives
aid and superintends, with zeal and singleness of
mind; he who does acts of mercy, with genuine
cheerfulness and joyful eagerness.

2 Corinthians 9:13 (AMP)

[13] Because at [your] standing of the test of this ministry, they will glorify God for your loyalty and obedience to the Gospel of Christ which you confess, as well as for your generous-hearted **liberality** to them and to all [the other needy ones].

Philippians 4:19 (AMP)

[19] And my God will **liberally** supply (fill to the full) your every need according to His riches in glory in Christ Jesus.

1 Timothy 6:17-19 (AMP)

[17] As for the rich in this world, charge them not to be proud and arrogant and contemptuous of others, nor to set their hopes on uncertain riches, but on God, Who richly and ceaselessly provides us with everything for [our] enjoyment.

[18] [Charge them] to do good, to be rich in good works, to be **liberal** and generous of heart, ready to share [with others],

[19] In this way laying up for themselves [the riches that endure forever as] a good foundation for the future, so that they may grasp that which is life indeed.

Paul is writing to Timothy here in regard to how the rich should be liberal and generous and ready to share with others, which rightly also lines up with what we read of the early church's governing of the people's money back in chapter 5, from the book of Acts, in which everyone shared all, which eliminated the needs of all. If we view this scripture example today regarding America's 2 major political parties, the more liberal Democrats and the conservative Republicans, which do you believe is governing more closely to Paul's words, the Democrats who would like to raise taxes on the rich back up to the levels of the past and cut war spending to help eliminate the needs of our nation's people, or the Republicans who believe that corporations and the rich should pay less tax, and America should spend more on defense for wars while having to cut many services for all of the nation's people from infrastructure for all people, to many services for the poor, sick and needy? Which party do you believe is governing closest to Paul's words?

> **James 1:5 (AMP)**
> [5] If any of you is deficient in wisdom, let him ask
> of the giving God [Who gives] to everyone
> **liberally** and ungrudgingly, without
> reproaching or faultfinding, and it will be given
> him.

Regarding the biblical definition of the word liberal, based on the 11 examples of it which we have just read, we can conclude with certainty that biblically, liberal is a very good word, and of the biblical examples which be, no one could rightfully argue against the simple fact, that being liberal has a lot to do with being very generous, to the point in which a couple of the examples could also conclude, that even God is a liberal giver. So now having researched the word liberal biblically, whether we liked the word or not in the past, we could all take as a very nice compliment from now on, if we are ever fortunate enough to be called a liberal, at least biblically. Liberal is a good word.

CHAPTER ELEVEN
A More Heavenly Government On Earth

At this point, we have seen beyond any doubt, that the bible has overwhelmingly proven to us, very conclusively and definitively, that the needs of all people being met are of absolute importance to God. All of this strong biblical evidence tells us without any further question, that any Christian politician or Christian leader in the world, or any Christian pastor, Christian teacher or Christian voter, who is against a government that works towards eliminating the basic needs of all people, is very obviously acting against the bible in which he or she professes to believe, it's that simple. Please don't shoot the messenger, the bible has spoken very loudly and clearly for itself, in regards to what the social justice of a nation should look like, all I have done is remind you of it.

So to briefly recap, and I'm speaking especially to the professed Christian politicians and Christian voters. If the early Christian church were in control of our government today, we would have the highest equivalent tax rates we've ever heard of, however there also wouldn't be any needy people among us, at all. Please think about this for a minute, church. No one hungry, no one homeless, no one whose medical needs weren't being completely tended to, no one with missing teeth, unless that's what they chose to do, no one behind on their utility bills, no one without the transportation they need to take them where they want to go, no one needing clothing, no one needing the massive funds for a really good education. Remember the early church Christians in chapter 5 from the book of Acts, for there was not a needy person found among them, and everyone shared as anyone might have need. There was nobody rich, and nobody poor, but everyone shared their talents and possessions alike, with gladness and sincerity of heart, and God's abundant grace was upon them all. Do you think they were happy? I have no doubt that these people were for the most part, extremely happy. No one had to worry about basic needs, and no one ever had to grieve over seeing others whose basic needs weren't being met. I believe that the early churches governing of the people's money in such a way as to eliminate the needs of all, had to be the closest example this world has ever seen to Jesus words "your kingdom come, your will be done, on earth as it is in heaven." This was the early Christian church example for the coming generations to observe and follow. This was the church which Jesus started and left for the world to see. Yes this is the true, the original biblical Christian church which cared enough about all of the people, to collectively share everything they had in order to eliminate the needs among them all. Welcome to true Christianity everyone. It loved the people more than money.

Do you believe heaven's government will operate in a similar way to the early church which Christ left for us? Why wouldn't it? However, we now have some 317,000,000 people in America today alone, and the many needs of the people don't just get taken care of by a few generous people, especially the needs of the most in need. Natural disasters are a good example of what is usually a very devastating scene that requires huge amounts of money, that only a government that operates much like the early Christian church can provide, in as short of time as possible, when the people really need help. No one could rightly believe that the victims of a natural disaster should just have to wait and see who will offer their own personal finances to try and help clean up a problem that is often times in the billions of dollars, that is ridiculous thinking. The vast majority of the people live much better when we can all work together for the common good through government, similar to what the early church did to eliminate needs. We simply can't have civilized nations without civilized governments that work for the vast majority of the people, and since we are talking bible politics, we now know without question, that the Christian church should be behind governments that resemble the governing of the people's money in working together for the common good of all, such as the early Christian church. This means being behind government services that work to make life better for the vast majority of the people, such as Social Security, Medicare, Medicaid, affordable healthcare for all and well-funded public education, among others. So when we hear politicians who want us to know they are Christian, and they talk about morals and family values these Christian politicians should be interested in strengthening these pillars of the American government just mentioned, but surely not making cuts to them.

This brings up one of the most important differences between America's capitalism and the early church. There is no biblical evidence of anyone making a profit from the distribution of any needs to the people in the early church's governing of the people's possessions and money. Maybe that is one good reason why the early church had no needy people, and America has so many, this is a really huge difference. Here are a few Old Testament examples that also agree with a government that would not be in business to make money off of the needs of the people, and God's blessing comes with it.

Deuteronomy 23:19-20 (NASB)

[19] "You shall not charge interest to your countrymen: interest on money, food, or anything that may be loaned at interest. [20] You may charge interest to a foreigner, but to your countrymen you shall not charge interest, so that the Lord your God may bless you in all that you undertake in the land which you are about to enter to possess.

Nehemiah 5:1-13 (NASB)

Usury Abolished

[1] Now there was a great outcry of the people and of their wives against their Jewish brothers. [2] For there were those who said, "We, our sons and our daughters are many; therefore let us get grain that we may eat and live." [3] There were others who said, "We are mortgaging our fields, our vineyards and our houses that we might get grain because of the

famine." [4] Also there were those who said, "We have borrowed money for the king's tax on our fields and our vineyards. [5] Now our flesh is like the flesh of our brothers, our children like their children. Yet behold, we are forcing our sons and our daughters to be slaves, and some of our daughters are forced into bondage already, and we are helpless because our fields and vineyards belong to others."

[6] Then I was very angry when I had heard their outcry and these words. [7] I consulted with myself and contended with the nobles and the rulers and said to them, "You are exacting usury, each from his brother!" Therefore, I held a great assembly against them. [8] I said to them, "We according to our ability have redeemed our Jewish brothers who were sold to the nations; now would you even sell your brothers that they may be sold to us?" Then they were silent and could not find a word to say. [9] Again I said, "The thing which you are doing is not good; should you not walk in the fear of our God because of the reproach of the nations, our enemies? [10] And likewise I, my brothers and my servants are lending them money and grain. Please, let us leave off this usury. [11] Please, give back to them this very day their fields, their vineyards, their olive groves and their houses, also the hundredth part of the money and of the grain, the new wine and the oil that you are exacting from them." [12] Then they said, "We will give it back and will require nothing from them; we will do

exactly as you say." So I called the priests and took
an oath from them that they would do according to
this promise. [13] I also shook out the front of my
garment and said, "Thus may God shake out every
man from his house and from his possessions who
does not fulfill this promise; even thus may he be
shaken out and emptied." And all the assembly said,
"Amen!" And they praised the Lord. Then the
people did according to this promise.

Usury is the practice of lending money at an exorbitant amount of interest.

Proverbs 28:8 (NASB)
[8] He who increases his wealth by interest and usury
Gathers it for him who is gracious to the poor.

So then, whether we look at the New Testament examples of the early
Christian church back in chapter 5, or these last 3 earlier Old Testament examples,
they would all agree with a no-profit government when it comes to the needs of
all people being met. How does this biblical governmental mindset equate into
our society today regarding what changes would have to be made within our
government, concerning the people's money, to line up as closely as possible to a
true biblical government? I believe based on all of the scriptural evidence which
we have seen, that we can say with absolute certainty, that true biblical
Christianity does lead us to know that everyone's money should be working
together in governments for the common good, of eliminating the basic needs of
all, in such a way that absolutely no one should be allowed to make a profit from
any service that is related to government. No profiteers of any kind in
government, but a government that is truly of the people, by the people, and for
the people. This would be a giant step towards true biblical Christianity. This
would be much more efficient in making the best possible services for all a reality,
and as reasonable as possible for everyone.

What would be the changes in American government that would truly make it a much more biblically correct government? This biblical governmental mindset would eliminate all for profit corporations from having any involvement in our government whatsoever, since corporations only have one goal, the goal to make as much profit for themselves as possible, and biblically this goal does not belong in our governments, since a biblically minded government is first and foremost about eliminating the basic needs of the people, not about feeding the desires of the extremely rich and their corporations. Of course the private sector has its place, but biblically its place isn't being involved with a nation's governmental decisions which are supposed to be about the people. A biblical government would stop profiteers from making money for themselves from government funds. There would be no more private for profit corporations linked to our government unless it was absolutely necessary in certain cases. But if possible, every governmental service would be simplified and as much corporate fat as possible would be removed. So as much as possible, there would be no more corporate profits for our countries people to have to pay for anything related to government. No more middlemen between the people and the government services. No corporate CEO bonuses for the tax payers to have to pay anymore, but the people would instead get more government services for their tax dollars. No more corporate campaign donations to any politician at all. And no more corporate lobbyists in congress paying off the politicians to give as much as possible to the corporations, and much less to the people. This would be a very big, very radical, and very biblically correct change, that would free up multitudes of tax dollars for services that the people really need. This would once again finally be an American government which would be of the people, by the people, and for the people again. This would be a government much closer to a biblical government.

At this point in America, it surely wouldn't be an easy fix, but if enough people organized and stood together in unity demanding it, I believe it could be accomplished, and we would be a giant biblical step closer to having a more heavenly government on earth.

So removing all corporations current ability to make decisions, regarding the governing of our nation's people's money, would be a colossal biblical step toward us coming much closer as a people, to having a more heavenly government on earth. Removing all of our American governments' huge corporate giveaways to big oil, big insurance, big banks, private war contractors and others, would most likely free up more than enough of the people's money (that's already there) to finally start doing what government is supposed to do biblically, to be all about serving the needs of the people. Things like free or very inexpensive healthcare could suddenly become a reality,. Excellent public education including free or very inexpensive college would also be no problem for the people to have anymore. Teacher's jobs would no longer be threatened, neither would police or firefighters jobs be threatened. There would be no more threats of cutting government services that the people have counted on for decades. Social Security, Medicare, and Medicaid could be permanently stronger than ever. And this biblically massive group of people (the poor, needy, hungry, helpless, orphan, afflicted, widow, fatherless, alien (immigrant) stranger and all who are oppressed) could suddenly have a much more heavenly peace than they did before.

What about Taxation?

Since I understand that nobody (in today's society) wants to give everything they have to eliminate the needs of all as the early Christian church did, this brings the question. Do you believe there should be a flat tax where the very poor person has to pay the same percentage of their income in tax as the billionaire, even though the poor person's health might be a very legitimate reason why they are poor? Or do you believe there should be a progressive tax system where the very poor pay nothing, and the more you make, the more you have to pay? I believe that Jesus has helped to answer this question for us here in Mark chapter 12.

> **Mark 12:41-44 (NASB)**
> **The Widow's Mite**
> [41] And He sat down opposite the treasury,

and began observing how the people
were putting money into the treasury; and many
rich people were putting in large sums. [42] A poor
widow came and put in two small copper coins,
which amount to a cent. [43] Calling His disciples to
Him, He said to them, "Truly I say to you, this poor
widow put in more than all the contributors to the
treasury; [44] for they all put in out of their surplus,
but she, out of her poverty, put in all she owned, all
she had to live on."

We should notice first that they were giving into the treasury, which would be like government today. Secondly, that even though this very poor widow only put in only a cent, Jesus said it was more than all the contributors put in the treasury because they all put in out of their surplus, but she, out of her poverty put in all she owned, all she had to live on. Obviously Jesus would not be for the idea of a flat tax, in taxing a person like a billionaire with the same percentage of their income as a middle class or very poor person, unless possibly the flat tax meant giving and sharing everything they had, as the early Christian church did. Is a flat tax fair when the very poor person has to pay all of their housing, food, utilities and possibly some day care among the rest on almost nothing, much of the time on an almost impossible minimum wage, and the very wealthy person often has millions and millions of dollars far beyond all of their living cost? So do you think the rich should have to pay a much higher percentage of their top income in tax than the middle class and the poor?

The Democrats and Republicans differ much on this issue, but let's take a look at history. If you have ever wondered in recent years what happened to the America you once knew, this may help to explain it to you. The numbers you are about to see are the historical highest marginal income tax rates for America's wealthiest people and wealthy corporations. These are the percentages they had to pay into the American government on their top income after deductions. Only those in the top one percent of America are represented by these numbers, millionaires and billionaires. These numbers are after the massive tax deductions and loopholes that the wealthiest people can take full advantages of. A special thanks to the Tax Policy Center, Urban Institute, Brookings Institution for the use of their work.

13-Apr-12

Historical Highest Marginal Income Tax Rates

Year	Top Marginal Rate	Year	Top Marginal Rate	Year	Top Marginal Rate
1913	7.0%	1947	86.45%	1981	69.13%
1914	7.0%	1948	82.13%	1982	50.00%
1915	7.0%	1949	82.13%	1983	50.00%
1916	15.0%	1950	91.00%	1984	50.00%
1917	67.0%	1951	91.00%	1985	50.00%
1918	77.0%	1952	92.00%	1986	50.00%
1919	73.0%	1953	92.00%	1987	38.50%
1920	73.0%	1954	91.00%	1988	28.00%
1921	73.0%	1955	91.00%	1989	28.00%
1922	56.0%	1956	91.00%	1990	31.00%
1923	56.0%	1957	91.00%	1991	31.00%
1924	46.0%	1958	91.00%	1992	31.00%
1925	25.0%	1959	91.00%	1993	39.60%
1926	25.0%	1960	91.00%	1994	39.60%
1927	25.0%	1961	91.00%	1995	39.60%
1928	25.0%	1962	91.00%	1996	39.60%
1929	24.0%	1963	91.00%	1997	39.60%
1930	25.0%	1964	77.00%	1998	39.60%
1931	25.0%	1965	70.00%	1999	39.60%
1932	63.0%	1966	70.00%	2000	39.60%
1933	63.0%	1967	70.00%	2001	38.60%
1934	63.0%	1968	75.25%	2002	38.60%
1935	63.0%	1969	77.00%	2003	35.00%
1936	79.0%	1970	71.75%	2004	35.00%
1937	79.0%	1971	70.00%	2005	35.00%
1938	79.0%	1972	70.00%	2006	35.00%
1939	79.0%	1973	70.00%	2007	35.00%
1940	81.10%	1974	70.00%	2008	35.00%
1941	81.00%	1975	70.00%	2009	35.00%
1942	88.00%	1976	70.00%	2010	35.00%
1943	88.00%	1977	70.00%	2011	35.00%
1944	94.00%	1978	70.00%	2012	35.00%
1945	94.00%	1979	70.00%		
1946	86.45%	1980	70.00%		

Note: Table contains a number of simplifications and ignores a number of factors, such as a maximum tax on earned income of 50 percent when the top rate was 70 percent and the current increase in rates due to income-related reductions in value of itemized deductions. Perhaps most importantly, it ignores the large increase in percentage of returns that were subject to this top rate.

Sources: Eugene Steuerle, The Urban Institute; Joseph Pechman, Federal Tax Policy; Joint Committee on Taxation, Summary of Conference Agreement on the Jobs and Growth Tax Relief Reconciliation Act of 2003, JCX-54-03, May 22, 2003; IRS Revised Tax Rate Schedules

It's interesting to think about America's last 100 years of tax history regarding the very rich and more interesting to consider how some of the events of America's history were very influenced by these numbers, and still are. For example, when we look back into the early 1900's it didn't take long for the American government to realize that very high rates of taxation on the wealthiest were very relevant to having a good economy. But shortly after the high tax rates on the wealthy had been initiated, these rates were brought back down into the 25% range in the early 1920's. You may recall what happened shortly after they lowered those tax rates down to the levels much like the wealthy are taxed at today, the great depression in 1929. You can also see in the 1930's how the tax rates on the wealthy were raised back up to 63% and stayed at least that high for about 50 years. You can see that during those years the top tax rates for the wealthiest Americans rose to as high as 94%.

If you are old enough you remember when America was the envy of the world, when it had a very fiscally healthy economy. America was booming and the American dream was a natural byproduct of America's healthy economy for most families. If the average person worked, they could have a great future. America's public schools were strong because they were well funded. America's roads had a lot less cracks and potholes, and you probably never heard about collapsing bridges in those days because America's infrastructure was well-funded and very strong. So these things and many others that are of extreme importance to us all were not neglected. Then you can see in the early 1980's during the Reagan administration, the tax rates on the wealthiest Americans which had been at least 63% for 50 years since the great depression were lowered from 70% at the beginning of the Reagan era, all the way down to the nearly pre great depression levels of 28% at the end of the Reagan era. America's economy was doomed to major fiscal problems from then on, and as you can see they haven't come back up much since. This has been a very massive amount of money that has been missing from the American government for about 30 years now, and America has especially felt the loss of it hard in recent years.

The American people desperately need these tax rates on the wealthiest Americans raised back up according to historical facts, yet the ever increasing wealthiest corporations and their political mouthpieces in Washington want us all to forget about this very important piece of history that strongly suggests America has a major lack of revenue problem. Yet their bought and paid for politicians in Washington will keep continuing to tell us that it's a spending problem that America has, you now know that history proves otherwise. Yet these people keep insisting that we need to cut the government services that help this biblical group of people. The poor, needy, hungry, helpless, orphan, afflicted, widow fatherless, alien (immigrant) stranger and all who are oppressed, among everyone else. The wealthiest one percent's wealth has increased very rapidly by not having to pay near as much into America's government. Arguably the wealthiest one percent of Americans now control at least 40% of America's wealth and growing rapidly.

A Very Rough Explanation of the Tax Numbers:

For the sake of understanding what these numbers mean, and to explain some major differences between the Democrat and Republican parties, we will pretend our money is pie for a moment. If the wealthiest one percent only have control of 40% of America's money, we could roughly explain it this way. If 100 of us were going to split 10 pies between us all, the wealthiest one of us who these numbers represent would get 4 of the 10 pies to him or herself. Then the remaining 99 of us would split the remaining 6 pies. This would leave the 99 of us with about 1/16th the slice of a whole pie. Realistically few of us would have a little more and most would have much less than the 1/16th.

One guy gets: 99 of us get:
O O O O (four pies)   v 1/16th of pie

Now let's think of it as our incomes for the year and we will see a major difference between the Democrat and Republican parties. The Republicans think that those of us with the tiny slice of pie should have to give up at least as much percent of it in tax as the super wealthy guy with the 4 pies. The Democrats think that the wealthy guy with 4 pies should have to give up a higher percentage of it in tax than the rest of us.

Doing What Actually Matters Biblically

Keeping our focus on bible politics, it is relevant for us to continue to consider this massive group of people whom we have read much scripture about that is near and dear to the heart of God. The poor, needy, hungry, helpless, orphan, afflicted, widow, fatherless, alien (immigrant) stranger and all who are oppressed by the oppressors. If we are serious about a more heavenly government on earth we will take God's word seriously concerning this group of people (who include most people at some point of our lives) with our political decisions as Christians, in voting to eliminate their needs as the early Christian church surely would have, by identifying and voting out the oppressors. Tax dollars from the wealthiest among us have everything to do with the will of God being done for this group of people.

As already mentioned, the Democrats and Republicans are completely opposite concerning this massive group of people. The Democrats desire to help these people more by taxing the wealthiest Americans with higher tax rates that are closer to the higher tax rates which the wealthiest Americans used to have to pay, because we truly have a lack of revenue problem. The Republicans are vehemently against raising tax rates on the wealthiest Americans at all, and instead continually strive to keep lowering the tax rates on the wealthy and the Republicans also desire to continually make huge cuts to the government services that help the poor, needy, hungry, helpless, orphan, afflicted, widow, fatherless, alien (immigrant) stranger and all who are oppressed because the Republicans say that we have a spending problem, at least they say this when it comes to the basic needs of the majority being met, yet in their eyes, there is always enough to give more huge tax breaks to the wealthiest Americans, which cost much more.

So the 2 parties' historical views are very different from one another, and it is a perfect recipe for never ending gridlock in Washington. The one thing about these differences between the Democrats and the Republicans is that the Democrats are far more in line with bible scripture on these matters, and the Republicans are very opposite in these matters of what true Christianity teaches. How sad that so many Republicans run as Christians while continually working against the poor, needy, hungry, helpless, orphan, afflicted, widow, fatherless, alien (immigrant) stranger and all who are oppressed. It would be impossible for me to say that the oppressors of these people are not the Republicans, because in America it is surely the Republicans doing nearly all the oppressing to this massive group of people. Do you believe that God is happy seeing the overwhelming majority of those who call themselves Christian in America voting for the Republican oppressors of the people?

To Protect God's Creation or Not?

If you are a Christian voter or Christian politician, you should believe this next scripture example from Revelation chapter 11, and you should believe that it is not only true, but that it is also going to happen someday. I bring this scripture example to your attention because I am always quite amazed when I've heard so many of my Christian friends talking against the E.P.A. Environmental Protection Agency, and talking against anyone who tries to regulate the big corporate polluters from being legally able to nearly run wild in their massive polluting of our air, water and soil. I always have to wonder if these people really honestly believe that God is against those who are trying to protect and care for His creation, all life and our planet? This scripture example alone should make you rethink your position and to change your thinking to being in line with your bible, to protect our environment as much as possible for the good of all forms of life that God has made. Notice the end of verse 18.

Revelation 11:15-18 (NASB)
The Seventh Trumpet—Christ's Reign Foreseen
[15] Then the seventh angel sounded; and there were loud voices in heaven, saying, "The kingdom of the world has become the kingdom of our Lord and of His Christ, and He will reign forever and ever." [16] And the twenty-four elders, who sit on their thrones before God, fell on their faces and worshiped God, [17] saying, "We give You thanks, O Lord God, the Almighty, who are and who were, because You have taken Your great power and have begun to reign. [18] And the nations were enraged, and Your wrath came, and the time came for the dead to be judged, and the time to reward Your bond-servants the prophets and the saints and those who fear Your name, the small and the great, and to destroy those who destroy the earth."

Who do you think are the destroyers of the earth? Do you believe the big polluters and oil companies might possibly fit into this scripture? How does this fit into our political choices of today? Which parties support less regulation and more polluting from these corporate giants of the earth?

The party in America that supports the corporations to pollute our air, water and soil much more is the Republican Party and the Democrats want to regulate the big polluters much more to slow their massive polluting. Nearly all of my Christian friends also support the Republican Party on this very important matter as well. This is very disturbing to me.

CHAPTER TWELVE
Scriptures Especially For the Church To Consider

Some Bible Politics Thoughts for the Church

We all as Christians have our political opinions, but can we as Christian voters or Christian politicians, prove our political opinions biblically? Are you sure? Are your political opinions as a Christian really based on bible scripture? Here is a common belief among many American churchgoers which the many bible scriptures in this book have proven to be a very false belief among the church. For many years I have heard many Christian people say things such as, that God wants us all to help people but HE didn't mean through government. I've always strongly disagreed with this kind of thinking, and you have now seen much scriptural proof that God is in fact for us having responsible governments for all people's best interest. Here are some of the things which I believe we can say are biblically correct, and in line with the politically relatable scriptures we have seen so far in Bible Politics.

1. The well-being of all people is of the highest importance to God.

2. A truly biblically correct government serves all people, and will attempt to eliminate (at very least) the basic needs of all, and the wealthiest should pay a higher percentage in tax on their income then the middle class and poor, to help make a biblically correct government a reality. I believe that we have not only proven this here biblically with much scripture, but we have also proven historically that the wealthiest people absolutely must be taxed much more again like times past, to achieve this. Democrats say yes to this need, Republicans vehemently oppose it, and instead keep insisting that we need to continually cut

more good government services that help the poor, needy, hungry, helpless, orphan, afflicted, widow, fatherless, alien (immigrant) stranger and all who are oppressed. The Democrats have already been proven, to be in a much more biblically correct position about this.

3. There were no such thing as corporations (in bible times) taking money away from the people, and preventing the early churches governing of the people's money to fully serve the people's needs. So whether you are a Christian politician, or a Christian voter, you should be in agreement with your bible to remove all corporate entities from government. We the people owe the corporations nothing, and we expect the most from our government services, and the only way to get the most government to all of its people, is to eliminate all for profit corporations from government once and for all. A truly biblically correct government will do this in the most efficient way possible for the good of all people, and will not allow private (for profit) corporate profiteers to make any more profit whatsoever on government services, which are supposed to be only for the needs of the people. A truly biblically correct government will provide the best services for all of its people in the most efficient way. Absolutely no profits for corporations that do nothing but interfere and obstruct a government's ability to provide the best services to the people. A Godly government will serve only its people, and not the corporations. We have seen enough bible scripture proving this.

4. We as God's church (if we regard our bible as true) should shake off any negative worldly interpretations of the word liberal which we have learned incorrectly that are in opposition to the true biblical definition of the word. Because biblically, God wants us to be generous liberal givers to others in need which represents the true biblical meaning of the word liberal. Liberal has been biblically proven to us in every example to be a very good word. The word liberal and its true biblical meaning actually gives respect in truth to the fact that America's political liberals of the past were the people who brought the very biblically correct governmental services to America such as Social Security,

Medicare, Medicaid and others, which to this day have been doing the will of God in lifting millions of people whom we all know out of the dire poverty which they would have been in, and used to be in, without these government services. They're biblically secure as being surely in the will of God.

We shall now look at more scripture examples, most of which are spoken by God through His prophets and apostles. For the most part, these are spoken as direction from God to His people with regard to the fact that God's people should care about the poor, needy and afflicted. I believe that the vast majority of America's church today is strongly lacking concern for the needs of the people, just like they were in some of these examples. If you still have not seen enough scripture to convince you, please consider these.

Jeremiah 5:26-31 (NASB)

26 'For wicked men are found among My people,
They watch like fowlers lying in wait;
They set a trap,
They catch men.
27 'Like a cage full of birds,
So their houses are full of deceit;
Therefore they have become great and rich.
28 'They are fat, they are sleek,
They also excel in deeds of wickedness;
They do not plead the cause,
The cause of the orphan, that they may prosper;
And they do not defend the rights of the poor.
29 'Shall I not punish these people?' declares
the Lord,
'On a nation such as this
Shall I not avenge Myself?'
30 "An appalling and horrible thing

Has happened in the land:
[31] The prophets prophesy falsely,
And the priests rule on their own authority;
And My people love it so!
But what will you do at the end of it?

The American Church Today

Today if we look at America's 2 major political parties, the Democrats and the Republicans, specifically to see which is most like the wicked men described in this scripture, the political party who votes against pleading the cause of the orphan, and votes against defending the rights of the poor, politically it is clearly the conservative and Tea Party Republicans who highly resemble these people whom God even declared "shall I not punish these people?" Yet the overwhelming majority of today's American churchgoers, their pastors and multitudes of others in ministry, get out in droves to religiously vote for these corporate conservative Republican politicians.

The world sees a church today that used to love people, now strongly united together in voting against such things as the affordable healthcare act, voting against helping the poor to have healthcare, which is surely not a very good witness for Christ, and surely doesn't appear to be a loving church to the world. These kind of decisions from the majority of the church only feed the oppressors (who we are supposed to be against) to have much more strength in their power to oppress the poor. It is somewhat amazing to me how the church has been given such an abundance of scripture that clearly makes working together for such things as affordable healthcare for all, an absolute no brainer, and without question the biblically right thing for a nation to do, yet it's getting harder all the time to find a pastor or anyone in the ministry today in America who is in favor of it. This is very disturbing to me and these things should not be happening among God's people.

So we have the bible which teaches us true Christianity in giving to those in need, then we have this thing that somehow crept its way into the church, that teaches us to believe that the poor and needy are burdens to society. It teaches us to be against good Godly government that serves them. It teaches us to believe that we should instead cut as much government funding for them as possible, in order to keep giving continually larger tax breaks to the wealthiest people and corporations who don't need it, and to keep spending more on ever increasing war spending. Essentially taking it all away from everyone from the middle class, to the most vulnerable and needy people of all ages among us. This thing they call conservative Christianity is surely a part of what has hurt America's economy and America's people.

So we have learned how the early Christian church's people shared everything they had to eliminate the needs of all, yet today's Christian church in America not only does not pay tax into the government, to help with the needs of all people, but it also preaches for the most part to vote for the conservative and Tea Party Republican oppressors, who create much more poverty among the people with their very fiscally unbiblical policies that are against the needs of the majority. This certainly appears to be the complete opposite of what we have now seen as true biblical Christianity, and as you just read in verse 31, God's people love it so, something opposite of true biblical Christianity in regards to the poor, and the vast majority of them still do.

I am not surprised in the least why so many Americans are for the separation of church and state, as I see God being so misrepresented by these politicians who legislate as haters of the needy, after they are elected as Christians, only to be reelected again, by the vast majority of the church.

Psalm 81:8-16 (NASB)
[8] "Hear, O My people, and I will admonish you;
O Israel, if you would listen to Me!
[9] "Let there be no strange god among you;
Nor shall you worship any foreign god.
[10] "I, the Lord, am your God,
Who brought you up from the land of Egypt;

Open your mouth wide and I will fill it.
[11] "But My people did not listen to My voice,
And Israel did not obey Me.
[12] "So I gave them over to the stubbornness of their
heart,
To walk in their own devices.
[13] "Oh that My people would listen to Me,
That Israel would walk in My ways!
[14] "I would quickly subdue their enemies
And turn My hand against their adversaries.
[15] "Those who hate the Lord would pretend
obedience to Him,
And their time of punishment would be forever.
[16] "But I would feed you with the finest of the
wheat,
And with honey from the rock I would satisfy you."

Regarding verse 9, I believe that the strange God today that is the root of most of our nation's troubles is the love of money, from the worldliest cases of it to also being very much within the church body.

Psalm 109:30-31 (NASB)

[30] With my mouth I will give thanks abundantly to
the Lord;
And in the midst of many I will praise Him.
[31] For He stands at the right hand of the needy,
To save him from those who judge his soul.

Christians shouldn't be judging the needy and voting against them. We are supposed to be a part of the solution, not the problem.

Proverbs 21:2-3 (NASB)

² Every man's way is right in his own eyes,

But the Lord weighs the hearts.

³ To do righteousness and justice

Is desired by the Lord more than sacrifice.

Isaiah 1:1-17 (NASB)

Rebellion of God's People

¹ The vision of Isaiah the son of Amoz

concerning Judah and Jerusalem, which he saw

during the reigns of Uzziah,

Jotham, Ahaz and Hezekiah, kings of Judah.

² Listen, O heavens, and hear, O earth;

For the Lord speaks,

"Sons I have reared and brought up,

But they have revolted against Me.

³ "An ox knows its owner,

And a donkey its master's manger,

But Israel does not know,

My people do not understand."

⁴ Alas, sinful nation,

People weighed down with iniquity,

Offspring of evildoers,

Sons who act corruptly!

They have abandoned the Lord,

They have despised the Holy One of Israel,

They have turned away from Him.

⁵ Where will you be stricken again,

As you continue in your rebellion?

The whole head is sick

And the whole heart is faint.

[6] From the sole of the foot even to the head

There is nothing sound in it,

Only bruises, welts and raw wounds,

Not pressed out or bandaged,

Nor softened with oil.

[7] Your land is desolate,

Your cities are burned with fire,

Your fields—strangers are devouring them in your presence;

It is desolation, as overthrown by strangers.

[8] The daughter of Zion is left like a shelter in a vineyard,

Like a watchman's hut in a cucumber field, like a besieged city.

[9] Unless the Lord of hosts

Had left us a few survivors,

We would be like Sodom,

We would be like Gomorrah.

God Has Had Enough

[10] Hear the word of the Lord,

You rulers of Sodom;

Give ear to the instruction of our God,

You people of Gomorrah.

[11] "What are your multiplied sacrifices to Me?"

Says the Lord.

"I have had enough of burnt offerings of rams

And the fat of fed cattle;

And I take no pleasure in the blood of bulls, lambs or goats.

[12] "When you come to appear before Me,

Who requires of you this trampling of My courts?
[13] "Bring your worthless offerings no longer,
Incense is an abomination to Me.
New moon and sabbath, the calling of assemblies—
I cannot endure iniquity and the solemn assembly.
[14] "I hate your new moon festivals and
your appointed feasts,
They have become a burden to Me;
I am weary of bearing them.
[15] "So when you spread out your hands in prayer,
I will hide My eyes from you;
Yes, even though you multiply prayers,
I will not listen.
Your hands are covered with blood.
[16] "Wash yourselves, make yourselves clean;
Remove the evil of your deeds from My sight.
Cease to do evil,
[17] Learn to do good;
Seek justice,
Reprove the ruthless,
Defend the orphan,
Plead for the widow.

Notice the things in verse 17 that are more important than church offerings to God, doing good, seeking justice, reproving the ruthless, defending the orphan, pleading for the widow. We have some 317 million people in America today, we need to vote for the party who wants to strengthen things like Social Security, Medicare, Medicaid, and affordable healthcare. The Democrats are in much better shape on this biblically than are the Republicans who strive to continually keep cutting these good government services for the people. Which political party do you believe is the ruthless? It is the Republicans in America who are insisting on ever increasing cuts to the government services with proven historical social justice to these groups of people that are so important to God. Where will we get the revenue for doing God's will? By taxing the corporations and wealthiest Americans again with tax rates that are much closer to the historical rates they used to pay in Chapter 11. And spending less on Defense. History proves this not only would bring our country back into good fiscal economical shape, but this would also be positively much closer to being biblically correct.

Isaiah 3:13-15 (NASB)
God Will Judge

[13] The Lord arises to contend,

And stands to judge the people.

[14] The Lord enters into judgment with the elders and

princes of His people,

"It is you who have devoured the vineyard;

The plunder of the poor is in your houses.

[15] "What do you mean by crushing My people

And grinding the face of the poor?"

Declares the Lord God of hosts.

Who are God's people? The poor are God's people according to Verse 15. Why do so many biblically educated people vote against the poor?

Isaiah 29:13-21 (NASB)

[13] Then the Lord said,

"Because this people draw near with their words

And honor Me with their lip service,

But they remove their hearts far from Me,

And their reverence for Me consists of tradition

learned by rote,

[14] Therefore behold, I will once again
deal marvelously with this people, wondrously
marvelous;
And the wisdom of their wise men will perish,
And the discernment of their discerning men will be
concealed."
[15] Woe to those who deeply hide their plans from
the Lord,
And whose deeds are done in a dark place,
And they say, "Who sees us?" or "Who knows us?"
[16] You turn things around!
Shall the potter be considered as equal with the
clay,
That what is made would say to its maker, "He did
not make me";
Or what is formed say to him who formed it, "He
has no understanding"?

Blessing after Discipline

[17] Is it not yet just a little while
Before Lebanon will be turned into a fertile field,
And the fertile field will be considered as a forest?
[18] On that day the deaf will hear words of a book,
And out of their gloom and darkness the eyes of the
blind will see.
[19] The afflicted also will increase their gladness in
the Lord,
And the needy of mankind will rejoice in the Holy
One of Israel.
[20] For the ruthless will come to an end and
the scorner will be finished,
Indeed all who are intent on doing evil will be cut
off;

²¹ Who cause a person to be indicted by a word,
And ensnare him who adjudicates at the gate,
And defraud the one in the right with meaningless
arguments.

I would much rather be on the side of the political party who is for helping the poor, needy and afflicted then to be with the ruthless scorners who are not concerned with them.

Isaiah 41:17 (NASB)

¹⁷ "The afflicted and needy are seeking water, but
there is none,
And their tongue is parched with thirst;
I, the Lord, will answer them Myself,
As the God of Israel I will not forsake them.

God will not forsake the afflicted and needy, so why do so many who call themselves Christian? Maybe they are not reading their bibles.

Isaiah 56:8-11 (NASB)

⁸ The Lord God, who gathers the dispersed of Israel,
declares,
"Yet others I will gather to them, to
those already gathered."
⁹ All you beasts of the field,
All you beasts in the forest,
Come to eat.
¹⁰ His watchmen are blind,
All of them know nothing.
All of them are mute dogs unable to bark,
Dreamers lying down, who love to slumber;

[11] And the dogs are greedy, they are not satisfied.

And they are shepherds who have no
understanding;

They have all turned to their own way,

Each one to his unjust gain, to the last one.

Shepherds are leaders of the church. God doesn't change, it's time for us as a church to remember what the heart of God is about. Church is supposed to be God's people, showing God's love to the people, and the people are supposed to be our business. The church shouldn't be siding with corporations, or being run like a corporation, not if it's about the people.

Isaiah 58:1-12 (NASB)
Observances of Fasts

[1] "Cry loudly, do not hold back;

Raise your voice like a trumpet,

And declare to My people their transgression

And to the house of Jacob their sins.

[2] "Yet they seek Me day by day and delight to know
My ways,

As a nation that has done righteousness

And has not forsaken the ordinance of their God.

They ask Me for just decisions,

They delight in the nearness of God.

[3] 'Why have we fasted and You do not see?

Why have we humbled ourselves and You do
not notice?'

Behold, on the day of your fast you
find your desire,

And drive hard all your workers.

[4] "Behold, you fast for contention and strife and to

strike with a wicked fist.
You do not fast like you do today to make your
voice heard on high.
[5] "Is it a fast like this which I choose, a day for a
man to humble himself?
Is it for bowing one's head like a reed
And for spreading out sackcloth and ashes as a bed?
Will you call this a fast, even an acceptable day to
the Lord?
[6] "Is this not the fast which I choose,
To loosen the bonds of wickedness,
To undo the bands of the yoke,
And to let the oppressed go free
And break every yoke?
[7] "Is it not to divide your bread with the hungry
And bring the homeless poor into the house;
When you see the naked, to cover him;
And not to hide yourself from your own flesh?
[8] "Then your light will break out like the dawn,
And your recovery will speedily spring forth;
And your righteousness will go before you;
The glory of the Lord will be your rear guard.
[9] "Then you will call, and the Lord will answer;
You will cry, and He will say, 'Here I am.'
If you remove the yoke from your midst,
The pointing of the finger and speaking wickedness,
[10] And if you give yourself to the hungry
And satisfy the desire of the afflicted,
Then your light will rise in darkness
And your gloom will become like midday.

¹¹ "And the Lord will continually guide you,
And satisfy your desire in scorched places,
And give strength to your bones;
And you will be like a watered garden,
And like a spring of water whose waters do not fail.
¹² "Those from among you will rebuild the ancient
ruins;
You will raise up the age-old foundations;
And you will be called the repairer of the breach,
The restorer of the streets in which to dwell.

Here is God speaking to Isaiah the prophet with a message for the people regarding fasting. Notice again the heart of God and some of the things that are obviously very important to God. These are things that should still be observed by the church as important to God. Starting in verse 6 and 7, God shows again how much he cares for the poor and the oppressed. He cares so much that if the Church does these things that God mentions in verses 6 and 7, that God will bless His people starting in verse 8 and 9. Notice God also doesn't like finger pointing from His church and speaking wickedness, which also apparently goes with finger pointing. In verse 10 God mentions again the importance of helping the hungry and to satisfy the desire of the afflicted. Then God promises good things to His people.

Who are the afflicted today? Many are those whose medical expenses are taking way too much of their money, as if their sickness alone wasn't already enough to bear for them, but they can't afford their bills because of it as well. It is shameful for today's church to vote against today's many afflicted people by voting against the Affordable Healthcare Act, Social Security, Medicare, Medicaid, and others, as they vote against good government by voting for the very anti-government conservative and Tea Party Republicans, which is voting against this example of God's will for the people.

Jeremiah 5:26-31 (NASB)

[26] 'For wicked men are found among My people,

They watch like fowlers lying in wait;

They set a trap,

They catch men.

[27] 'Like a cage full of birds,

So their houses are full of deceit;

Therefore they have become great and rich.

[28] 'They are fat, they are sleek,

They also excel in deeds of wickedness;

They do not plead the cause,

The cause of the orphan, that they may prosper;

And they do not defend the rights of the poor.

[29] 'Shall I not punish these people?' declares

the Lord,

'On a nation such as this

Shall I not avenge Myself?'

[30] "An appalling and horrible thing

Has happened in the land:

[31] The prophets prophesy falsely,

And the priests rule on their own authority;

And My people love it so!

But what will you do at the end of it?

You have already seen this scripture example at the beginning of this chapter. I personally will never be able to understand how any leader in ministry could read scriptures like this one and the many others in this book and continue to vote against defending the rights of the poor by voting against such things as the Affordable Healthcare Act. You pastors and leaders in the church who do such things are clearly voting against your own bibles in which you preach. You are keeping many people from wanting to know God. This is really a shame.

Jeremiah 6:1-21 (NASB)

Destruction of Jerusalem Impending

[1] "Flee for safety, O sons of Benjamin,

From the midst of Jerusalem!

Now blow a trumpet in Tekoa

And raise a signal over Beth-haccerem;

For evil looks down from the north,

And a great destruction.

[2] "The comely and dainty one, the daughter of Zion,

I will cut off.

[3] "Shepherds and their flocks will come to her,

They will pitch their tents around her,

They will pasture each in his place.

[4] "Prepare war against her;

Arise, and let us attack at noon.

Woe to us, for the day declines,

For the shadows of the evening lengthen!

[5] "Arise, and let us attack by night

And destroy her palaces!"

[6] For thus says the Lord of hosts,

"Cut down her trees

And cast up a siege against Jerusalem.

This is the city to be punished,

In whose midst there is only oppression.

[7] "As a well keeps its waters fresh,

So she keeps fresh her wickedness.

Violence and destruction are heard in her;

Sickness and wounds are ever before Me.

[8] "Be warned, O Jerusalem,

Or I shall be alienated from you,

And make you a desolation,

A land not inhabited."

[9] Thus says the Lord of hosts,

"They will thoroughly glean as the vine the remnant of Israel;

Pass your hand again like a grape gatherer

Over the branches."

[10] To whom shall I speak and give warning

That they may hear?

Behold, their ears are closed

And they cannot listen.

Behold, the word of the Lord has become a reproach to them;

They have no delight in it.

[11] But I am full of the wrath of the Lord;

I am weary with holding it in.

"Pour it out on the children in the street

And on the gathering of young men together;

For both husband and wife shall be taken,

The aged and the very old.

[12] "Their houses shall be turned over to others,

Their fields and their wives together;

For I will stretch out My hand

Against the inhabitants of the land," declares the Lord.

[13] "For from the least of them even to the greatest of them,

Everyone is greedy for gain,

And from the prophet even to the priest

Everyone deals falsely.

[14] "They have healed the brokenness of My people superficially,

Saying, 'Peace, peace,'
But there is no peace.
¹⁵ "Were they ashamed because of the abomination
they have done?
They were not even ashamed at all;
They did not even know how to blush.
Therefore they shall fall among those who fall;
At the time that I punish them,
They shall be cast down," says the Lord.
¹⁶ Thus says the Lord,
"Stand by the ways and see and ask for the ancient
paths,
Where the good way is, and walk in it;
And you will find rest for your souls.
But they said, 'We will not walk in it.'
¹⁷ "And I set watchmen over you, saying,
'Listen to the sound of the trumpet!'
But they said, 'We will not listen.'
¹⁸ "Therefore hear, O nations,
And know, O congregation, what is among them.
¹⁹ "Hear, O earth: behold, I am bringing disaster on
this people,
The fruit of their plans,
Because they have not listened to My words,
And as for My law, they have rejected it also.
²⁰ "For what purpose does frankincense come to Me
from Sheba
And the sweet cane from a distant land?
Your burnt offerings are not acceptable
And your sacrifices are not pleasing to Me."
²¹ Therefore, thus says the Lord,

"Behold, I am laying stumbling blocks before this
people.
And they will stumble against them,
Fathers and sons together;
Neighbor and friend will perish."

If God was against responsible governments for all people, that provide at very least a good education for everyone and free or very reasonable healthcare, He would never have said such things as this, nor would this kind of thing have made Him very upset. The first thing that He says about the city of Jerusalem was that there was only oppression there. He continues to say in verse 7 that she keeps fresh her wickedness. Violence and destruction are heard in her; sickness and wounds are ever before me, He said.

This sounds much more like a place that does not care for its people than one that does. This sounds much more like a bare bones conservative government than one that gives liberally to its people as we are supposed to. In verse 13 we see that everyone was greedy for gain, even the prophets and priest, and they wouldn't listen to God. Do you think the church is listening to God with their bibles today politically? They are giving their offerings to the church, but we have seen many examples that prove God isn't near as interested in their sacrifices, as He is interested in them treating the people right, by doing away with the oppressors. Voting them out.

Jeremiah 7:1-7 (NASB)
Message at the Temple Gate
[1] The word that came to Jeremiah from the Lord, saying, [2] "Stand in the gate of the Lord's house and proclaim there this word and say, 'Hear the word of the Lord, all you of Judah, who enter by these gates to worship the Lord!'" [3] Thus says the Lord of hosts, the God of Israel, "Amend your ways and

your deeds, and I will let you dwell in this
place. ⁴Do not trust in deceptive words, saying,
'This is the temple of the Lord, the temple of
the Lord, the temple of the Lord.'⁵For if you truly
amend your ways and your deeds, if you
truly practice justice between a man and his
neighbor, ⁶if you do not oppress the alien,
the orphan, or the widow, and do not shed innocent
blood in this place, nor walk after other gods to
your own ruin, ⁷then I will let you dwell in this
place, in the land that I gave to your fathers forever
and ever.

The problems with the oppression of the people and the church supporting the oppressors are obviously nothing new. If God wasn't happy about it then, we can be assured that he's probably not very happy about it now. Again God is telling them to change, and what is God wanting here? God wants justice for all and He does not want oppression on the alien (immigrant), orphan or widow. He also wants the shedding of innocent blood to stop, and not to walk after other Gods (like money) to your own ruin. Notice God told His people that if they did these things, He would let them dwell there in the land that He gave to their fathers forever and ever.

How many Christians vote against the oppressors today? Not near enough. If we as Christians really do care as God wants us to, for people, then we should care a lot about protecting Social Security, Medicare, Medicaid, and the Affordable Healthcare Act among others that protect the most vulnerable people who have been dealt the worst in life. The traditional Democrats win big here over the Republicans, but if there are Democrats that side with the Republicans to cut these services, then we must also vote out these oppressing Democrats as well as the Republicans.

Jeremiah 8:4-12 (NASB)

[4] "You shall say to them, 'Thus says the Lord,

"Do men fall and not get up again?

Does one turn away and not repent?

[5] "Why then has this people, Jerusalem,

Turned away in continual apostasy?

They hold fast to deceit,

They refuse to return.

[6] "I have listened and heard,

They have spoken what is not right;

No man repented of his wickedness,

Saying, 'What have I done?'

Everyone turned to his course,

Like a horse charging into the battle.

[7] "Even the stork in the sky

Knows her seasons;

And the turtledove and the swift and the thrush

Observe the time of their migration;

But My people do not know

The ordinance of the Lord.

[8] "How can you say, 'We are wise,

And the law of the Lord is with us'?

But behold, the lying pen of the scribes

Has made it into a lie.

[9] "The wise men are put to shame,

They are dismayed and caught;

Behold, they have rejected the word of the Lord,

And what kind of wisdom do they have?

[10] "Therefore I will give their wives to others,

Their fields to new owners;

Because from the least even to the greatest

Everyone is greedy for gain;
From the prophet even to the priest
Everyone practices deceit.
[11] "They heal the brokenness of the daughter of My
people superficially,
Saying, 'Peace, peace,'
But there is no peace.
[12] "Were they ashamed because of the abomination
they had done?
They certainly were not ashamed,
And they did not know how to blush;
Therefore they shall fall among those who fall;
At the time of their punishment they shall be
brought down,"
Says the Lord.

God again shows that He is upset with His people. God's people long ago were acting much like the majority of America's Christians today against the poor and needy. They were not listening to God's word then, and I have to believe based on their majority voting for the conservative oppressors today, that they surely aren't listening to God's word much more today concerning the needy. Voting for the conservative and Tea Party Republicans who have tried very hard, 40 times to take away affordable healthcare from everyone puts today's church in an equal place with those of the past who allowed oppression to reign in their land. We need to tax the wealthy again as in the days of old. Democrats strongly agree, Republicans couldn't disagree more than they do.

Jeremiah 22:1-9 (NASB)
Warning of Jerusalem's Fall
[1] Thus says the Lord, "Go down to the house of the
king of Judah, and there speak this word [2] and say,

'Hear the word of the Lord, O king of Judah,
who sits on David's throne, you and your servants
and your people who enter these gates. ³ Thus says
the Lord, "Do justice and righteousness, and deliver
the one who has been robbed from the power of
his oppressor. Also do not mistreat or do violence to
the stranger, the orphan, or the widow; and do
not shed innocent blood in this place. ⁴ For if you
men will indeed perform this thing, then kings will
enter the gates of this house, sitting in David's place
on his throne, riding in chariots and on horses, even
the king himself and his servants and his
people.⁵ But if you will not obey these words,
I swear by Myself," declares the Lord, "that this
house will become a desolation."'" ⁶ For thus says
the Lord concerning the house of the king of Judah:

> "You are like Gilead to Me,
> Like the summit of Lebanon;
> Yet most assuredly I will make you like
> a wilderness,
> Like cities which are not inhabited.
> ⁷ "For I will set apart destroyers against you,
> Each with his weapons;
> And they will cut down your choicest cedars
> And throw them on the fire.

⁸ "Many nations will pass by this city; and they
will say to one another, 'Why has the Lord done
thus to this great city?'⁹ Then they will answer,
'Because they forsook the covenant of
the Lord their God and bowed down to other gods
and served them.'"

When we see how God tried to warn His people who didn't listen to Him, is it any wonder when they lose their land to others today? This is not rocket science, it's about good government, it's about treating all of the people rightly, with the care and respect they deserve, this is how God always wanted it. America is quickly becoming a desolation as in verse 5. America who always spends more for shedding innocent blood in more wars, while cutting good government services which the people really need from Social Security to public education. We don't need to cut anything, we need to make these government services work much more for the people by cutting war spending and taxing the wealthiest Americans to the high levels of old again.

Amos 8:1-12 (NASB)
Basket of Fruit and Israel's Captivity

[1] Thus the Lord God showed me, and behold, there was a basket of summer fruit. [2] He said, "What do you see, Amos?" And I said, "A basket of summer fruit." Then the Lord said to me, "The end has come for My people Israel. I will spare them no longer. [3] The songs of the palace will turn to wailing in that day," declares the Lord God. "Many will be the corpses; in every place they will cast them forth in silence."

[4] Hear this, you who trample the needy, to do away with the humble of the land, [5] saying,

> "When will the new moon be over,
> So that we may sell grain,
> And the sabbath, that we may open the wheat market,
> To make the bushel smaller and the shekel bigger,
> And to cheat with dishonest scales,

⁶ So as to buy the helpless for money
And the needy for a pair of sandals,
And that we may sell the refuse of the
wheat?"
⁷ The Lord has sworn by the pride of Jacob,
"Indeed, I will never forget any of their
deeds.
⁸ "Because of this will not the land quake
And everyone who dwells in it mourn?
Indeed, all of it will rise up like the Nile,
And it will be tossed about
And subside like the Nile of Egypt.
⁹ "It will come about in that day," declares
the Lord God,
"That I will make the sun go down at noon
And make the earth dark in broad daylight.
¹⁰ "Then I will turn your festivals into
mourning
And all your songs into lamentation;
And I will bring sackcloth on everyone's
loins
And baldness on every head.
And I will make it like a time of mourning
for an only son,
And the end of it will be like a bitter day.
¹¹ "Behold, days are coming," declares the
Lord God,
"When I will send a famine on the land,
Not a famine for bread or a thirst for water,
But rather for hearing the words of the Lord.
¹² "People will stagger from sea to sea

And from the north even to the east;

They will go to and fro to seek the word of

the Lord,

But they will not find it.

Look who the first people were whom God spoke of, after He told Amos that the end had come for His people Israel. After He said that He would spare them no more. In verse 4, it was against those who trample the needy, to do away with the humble of the land. Who are these politicians today? It is absolutely the conservative Republicans and the even more conservative Republican Tea Party. The vast majority of America's church stands behind these political oppressors who continually trample the needy only to give it all to the wealthiest in ever increasing tax breaks. Corporate welfare is so much more expensive than the kind that our bibles tell us to be concerned with, for the needs of the majority, to stop poverty. God wants us to act as though we have heard His words and quit making more needy people with our political decisions

Zephaniah 3 (NASB)
Woe to Jerusalem and the Nations

[1] Woe to her who is rebellious and defiled,

The tyrannical city!

[2] She heeded no voice,

She accepted no instruction.

She did not trust in the Lord,

She did not draw near to her God.

[3] Her princes within her are roaring lions,

Her judges are wolves at evening;

They leave nothing for the morning.

[4] Her prophets are reckless, treacherous men;

Her priests have profaned the sanctuary.

They have done violence to the law.

[5] The Lord is righteous within her;
He will do no injustice.
Every morning He brings His justice to light;
He does not fail.
But the unjust knows no shame.
[6] "I have cut off nations;
Their corner towers are in ruins.
I have made their streets desolate,
With no one passing by;
Their cities are laid waste,
Without a man, without an inhabitant.
[7] "I said, 'Surely you will revere Me,
Accept instruction.'
So her dwelling will not be cut off
According to all that I have appointed concerning her.
But they were eager to corrupt all their deeds.
[8] "Therefore wait for Me," declares the Lord,
"For the day when I rise up as a witness.
Indeed, My decision is to gather nations,
To assemble kingdoms,
To pour out on them My indignation,
All My burning anger;
For all the earth will be devoured
By the fire of My zeal.
[9] "For then I will give to the peoples purified lips,
That all of them may call on the name of the Lord,
To serve Him shoulder to shoulder.
[10] "From beyond the rivers of Ethiopia
My worshipers, My dispersed ones,
Will bring My offerings.

[11] "In that day you will feel no shame
Because of all your deeds
By which you have rebelled against Me;
For then I will remove from your midst
Your proud, exulting ones,
And you will never again be haughty
On My holy mountain.

A Remnant of Israel

[12] "But I will leave among you
A humble and lowly people,
And they will take refuge in the name of the Lord.
[13] "The remnant of Israel will do no wrong
And tell no lies,
Nor will a deceitful tongue
Be found in their mouths;
For they will feed and lie down
With no one to make them tremble."
[14] Shout for joy, O daughter of Zion!
Shout in triumph, O Israel!
Rejoice and exult with all your heart,
O daughter of Jerusalem!
[15] The Lord has taken away His judgments against
you,
He has cleared away your enemies.
The King of Israel, the Lord, is in your midst;
You will fear disaster no more.
[16] In that day it will be said to Jerusalem:
"Do not be afraid, O Zion;
Do not let your hands fall limp.
[17] "The Lord your God is in your midst,
A victorious warrior.

He will exult over you with joy,

He will be quiet in His love,

He will rejoice over you with shouts of joy.

[18] "I will gather those who grieve about the

appointed feasts—

They came from you, O Zion;

The reproach of exile is a burden on them.

[19] "Behold, I am going to deal at that time

With all your oppressors,

I will save the lame

And gather the outcast,

And I will turn their shame into praise and renown

In all the earth.

[20] "At that time I will bring you in,

Even at the time when I gather you together;

Indeed, I will give you renown and praise

Among all the peoples of the earth,

When I restore your fortunes before your eyes,"

Says the Lord.

Many world leaders claim to be Christian but do their deeds line up with what God wants from them? Do they work for all of the people to attempt to prevent poverty and to move the nation's people forward into a life of hope, so that their hard work can pay off and that they can have a good life? Or do they vote against the vast majority of the people's best interest and in so doing, create more poor and needy people?

Someday God will remove the proud and the exulting ones and He will leave a humble and lowly people, these people will do no wrong and tell no lies. They will have peace because God will deal with all of the oppressors. So what kind of people should our leaders be? We should have leaders that don't mind taxing the wealthiest enough again to stop the oppression once and for all.

Complete healthcare for all for starters. And if America would start making significant cuts to defense spending for more wars, we could still be way ahead of the other nations in defense, plus we could have a decent nation again without making any cuts to infrastructure, Social Security, Medicare, Medicaid, affordable healthcare for all, education, etc. This is not rocket science. We just need to vote out all of the politicians who oppose these time tested proven solutions.

Corporate welfare is so much more expensive for a nation's people to pay, then welfare for the good of all people. It's much less expensive for a nation to tax the wealthy again for the good of all people. Your vote is not about ending welfare, it's about who gets the welfare. Democrats and Republicans. Welfare for all including the needy, or welfare for the greedy, to tax the rich or not, that is the difference.

> **Zechariah 7:4-14**
> **New American Standard Bible (NASB)**
> [4] Then the word of the Lord of hosts came to me, saying, [5] "Say to all the people of the land and to the priests, 'When you fasted and mourned in the fifth and seventh months these seventy years, was it actually for Me that you fasted? [6] When you eat and drink, do you not eat for yourselves and do you not drink for yourselves? [7] Are not these the words which the Lord proclaimed by the former prophets, when Jerusalem was inhabited and prosperous along with its cities around it, and the Negev and the foothills were inhabited?'"
> [8] Then the word of the Lord came to Zechariah saying, [9] "Thus has the Lord of hosts said, 'Dispense true justice and practice kindness and compassion each to his brother; [10] and do not oppress the widow or the orphan, the stranger or the

poor; and do not devise evil in your hearts against one another.' [11] But they refused to pay attention and turned a stubborn shoulder and stopped their ears from hearing. [12] They made their hearts like flint so that they could not hear the law and the words which the Lord of hosts had sent by His Spirit through the former prophets; therefore great wrath came from the Lord of hosts. [13] And just as He called and they would not listen, so they called and I would not listen," says the Lord of hosts; [14] "but I scattered them with a storm wind among all the nations whom they have not known. Thus the land is desolated behind them so that no one went back and forth, for they made the pleasant land desolate."

How can anyone who is a leader in the church be serious when they say such things as that God didn't mean for governments to help the people? How can these people be serious? When is the last time they opened their bibles? It is said recently that the top 400 wealthiest Americans now have more money than America's bottom 150 million people combined, that's almost one half of our nation's people. America has too many millionaires in congress making laws that oppress the majority and continually make these 400 people all the wealthier. You should certainly have seen enough scripture by now to know that this is a country that is extremely far from the will of God. Regarding this scripture, we can see again what is important to God in verse 9 and 10. And in verse 11 how His people didn't listen to Him. Instead they were stubborn and refused to pay attention to Him, just like now.

Oppression is always on the rise today and the church could be a big part of changing this if they would vote for the politicians who want a good strong government for the people again like we used to have. Today that means voting for almost all of the Democrats, and none of the Republicans that I am aware of. The Republican politicians' voting records speak loudly against the people and themselves.

> **Malachi 3:1-5 (NASB)**
> **The Purifier**
> [1] "Behold, I am going to send My messenger, and he will clear the way before Me. And the Lord, whom you seek, will suddenly come to His temple; and the messenger of the covenant, in whom you delight, behold, He is coming," says the Lord of hosts. [2] "But who can endure the day of His coming? And who can stand when He appears? For He is like a refiner's fire and like fullers' soap. [3] He will sit as a smelter and purifier of silver, and He will purify the sons of Levi and refine them like gold and silver, so that they may present to the Lord offerings in righteousness. [4] Then the offering of Judah and Jerusalem will be pleasing to the Lord as in the days of old and as in former years.
> [5] "Then I will draw near to you for judgment; and I will be a swift witness against the sorcerers and against the adulterers and against those who swear falsely, and against those who oppress the wage earner in his wages, the widow and the orphan, and those who turn aside the alien and do not fear Me," says the Lord of hosts.

Verse 5. Who is against raising the unlivable minimum wage? It is the Republican Party. Who is for raising the minimum wage to a livable wage? The

Democrats are, or at least most of them, and if any of them vote along with the Republican oppressors we need to also vote them out ASAP.

Who is for the oppressive sequester cuts? It is the Republicans, including the Tea Party Republicans. Who is very against the oppressive sequester cuts? The Democrats are against the sequester because it is terrible for the people.

> **Romans 16:17-18 (NASB)**
> [17] Now I urge you, brethren, keep your eye on those
> who cause dissensions and hindrances contrary to
> the teaching which you learned, and turn away from
> them. [18] For such men are slaves, not of our Lord
> Christ but of their own appetites; and by
> their smooth and flattering speech they deceive the
> hearts of the unsuspecting.

We are either politically loving people more or loving money more. A preacher who loves money instead of people isn't qualified to preach. If they are against things such as affordable healthcare for all, they have disqualified themselves biblically without question. Maybe it's time for America to start taxing the larger churches again if the church leaders refuse to change on this important issue.

> **Ephesians 4:17-19 (NASB)**
> **The Christian's Walk**
> [17] So this I say, and affirm together with the
> Lord, that you walk no longer just as the Gentiles
> also walk, in the futility of their
> mind, [18] being darkened in their
> understanding, excluded from the life of God
> because of the ignorance that is in them, because of
> the hardness of their heart; [19] and they,

having become callous, have given themselves over
to sensuality for the practice of every kind of
impurity with greediness.

Here is a very good description of the person in ministry who is against good government which provides basics such as affordable healthcare for all and good public education. As Christians we should always be mindful not to be greedy. Are we loving people more or money in our voting?

Philippians 3:17-19 (NASB)
[17] Brethren, join in following my example, and
observe those who walk according to the pattern
you have in us. [18] For many walk, of whom I often
told you, and now tell you even weeping, that they
are enemies of the cross of Christ,[19] whose end is
destruction, whose god is their appetite,
and whose glory is in their shame, who set their
minds on earthly things.

1 Timothy 6:3-11 (AMP)
[3] But if anyone teaches otherwise and does
not assent to the sound and wholesome messages of
our Lord Jesus Christ (the Messiah) and the
teaching which is in agreement with godliness
(piety toward God),
[4] He is puffed up with pride and stupefied with
conceit, [although he is] woefully ignorant. He has
a morbid fondness for controversy and
disputes and strife about words, which result in
(produce) envy and jealousy, quarrels and
dissension, abuse *and* insults and slander, and base
suspicions,

⁵ And protracted wrangling and wearing discussion and perpetual friction among men who are corrupted in mind and bereft of the truth, who imagine that godliness or righteousness is a source of profit [a moneymaking business, a means of livelihood]. From such withdraw.

⁶ [And it is, indeed, a source of immense profit, for] godliness accompanied with contentment (that contentment which is a sense of inward sufficiency) is great and abundant gain.

⁷ For we brought nothing into the world, and obviously we cannot take anything out of the world;

⁸ But if we have food and clothing, with these we shall be content (satisfied).

⁹ But those who crave to be rich fall into temptation and a snare and into many foolish (useless, godless) and hurtful desires that plunge men into ruin and destruction and miserable perishing.

¹⁰ For the love of money is a root of all evils; it is through this craving that some have been led astray and have wandered from the faith and pierced themselves through with many acute [mental] pangs.

¹¹ But as for you, O man of God, flee from all these things; aim at and pursue righteousness (right standing with God and true goodness), godliness (which is the loving fear of God and being Christlike), faith, love, steadfastness (patience), and gentleness of heart.

2 Timothy 3:1-7Translation (GW)
Watch Out for Sinful People

[1] You must understand this: In the last days there will be violent periods of time. [2] People will be selfish and love money. They will brag, be arrogant, and use abusive language. They will curse their parents, show no gratitude, have no respect for what is holy, [3] and lack normal affection for their families. They will refuse to make peace with anyone. They will be slanderous, lack self-control, be brutal, and have no love for what is good. [4] They will be traitors. They will be reckless and conceited. They will love pleasure rather than God. [5] They will appear to have a godly life, but they will not let its power change them. Stay away from such people. [6] Some of these men go into homes and mislead weak-minded women who are burdened with sins and led by all kinds of desires. [7] These women are always studying but are never able to recognize the truth.

2 Timothy 3:12-17 (GW)

[12] Those who try to live a godly life because they believe in Christ Jesus will be persecuted. [13] But evil people and phony preachers will go from bad to worse as they mislead people and are themselves misled.

[14] However, continue in what you have learned and found to be true. You know who your teachers were. [15] From infancy you have known the Holy Scriptures. They have the power to give you

wisdom so that you can be saved through faith in Christ Jesus. [16] Every Scripture passage is inspired by God. All of them are useful for teaching, pointing out errors, correcting people, and training them for a life that has God's approval. [17] They equip God's servants so that they are completely prepared to do good things.

Titus 1:10-11 (NKJV)
The Elders' Task
[10] For there are many insubordinate, both idle talkers and deceivers, especially those of the circumcision, [11] whose mouths must be stopped, who subvert whole households, teaching things which they ought not, for the sake of dishonest gain.

Titus 1:15-16 (NASB)
[15] To the pure, all things are pure; but to those who are defiled and unbelieving, nothing is pure, but both their mind and their conscience are defiled. [16] They profess to know God, but by their deeds they deny Him, being detestable and disobedient and worthless for any good deed.

Hebrews 5:11-14 (GW)
You Need Someone to Teach You
[11] We have a lot to explain about this. But since you have become too lazy to pay attention, explaining it to you is hard. [12] By now you should be teachers. Instead, you still need someone to teach you the elementary truths of God's word. You need milk,

not solid food. ¹³ All those who live on milk lack the experience to talk about what is right. They are still babies. ¹⁴ However, solid food is for mature people, whose minds are trained by practice to know the difference between good and evil.

2 Peter 2:1-3 (NASB)
The Rise of False Prophets

¹ But false prophets also arose among the people, just as there will also be false teachers among you, who will secretly introduce destructive heresies, even denying the Master who bought them, bringing swift destruction upon themselves. ² Many will follow their sensuality, and because of them the way of the truth will be maligned; ³ and in their greed they will exploit you with false words; their judgment from long ago is not idle, and their destruction is not asleep.

2 Peter 3:10-18 (NASB)
A New Heaven and Earth

¹⁰ But the day of the Lord will come like a thief, in which the heavens will pass away with a roar and the elements will be destroyed with intense heat, and the earth and its works will be burned up. ¹¹ Since all these things are to be destroyed in this way, what sort of people ought you to be in holy conduct and godliness, ¹² looking for and hastening the coming of the day of God, because of which the heavens will be destroyed by burning, and the elements will melt with intense heat! ¹³ But

according to His promise we are looking for new
heavens and a new earth, in which righteousness
dwells.
¹⁴ Therefore, beloved, since you look for these
things, be diligent to be found by Him in
peace, spotless and blameless,¹⁵ and regard
the patience of our Lord as salvation; just as
also our beloved brother Paul, according to the
wisdom given him, wrote to you, ¹⁶ as also in
all his letters, speaking in them of these things, in
which are some things hard to understand, which
the untaught and unstable distort, as they do also the
rest of the Scriptures, to their own
destruction. ¹⁷ You therefore, beloved, knowing this
beforehand, be on your guard so that you are not
carried away by the error of unprincipled men
and fall from your own steadfastness, ¹⁸ but grow in
the grace and knowledge of our Lord and Savior
Jesus Christ. To Him be the glory, both now and to
the day of eternity. Amen.

Bible Politics was written primarily to prove to the Christian voters and Christian politicians that there are some pretty major differences between true biblical Christianity and today's corporate conservative Christianity.

What would Jesus do? The church so often asks. The answer to this question is most often going to be found when we actually look at what Jesus did do, and sometimes even more importantly, what Jesus didn't do. We have not only done this concerning Jesus in Bible Politics, but have also searched the entire bible cover to cover, in relation to political matters. As you have been reading *Bible Politics*, it has become clearly evident to you, and has been proven over and over and over, that God has absolutely not agreed with much of His American church today when they vote against government services which greatly reduce poverty and other forms of oppression, like the Affordable Healthcare Act, Social Security, Medicare, Medicaid, and other forms of government that greatly reduce need among the majority including the poor, needy, and afflicted.

The many scriptures in Bible Politics have proven to these Christian politicians, pastors, teachers and Christian voters, that God is much more in favor of governments which help with these services for the people, such as free or very reasonable healthcare for all, good public education and others and He is not against them. God is for them in a big way, and absolutely not against a government that helps all the people with these things. I do realize that I have sounded very repetitive throughout the book, as the bible proved over and over to be in great favor of governments that do work towards the benefit of all people in various ways to eliminate poverty. So in reiterating all of these powerful scriptures which strongly made the case by themselves, it simply came naturally to have to be very repetitive in doing so.

I believe that every reader of *Bible Politics* has been surprised with how many scripture examples the bible has in support of good government for the people. I also believe that many of the readers have learned that God isn't at all who they thought He was. But instead they have learned that God is very generous, and God is not the cheapskate God who has been so grossly misrepresented politically by so many Christian talking politicians, who just can't seem to wait to make ever increasing cuts to the good government services for the majority, including the poorest, neediest, and most afflicted. No, that is not a politician who is representing the true God of the bible, because God wants mercy and justice for everyone. Instead these politicians are representing this man made cheapskate conservative God who is not represented in our bibles.

I assure you that I did not write this book to tell anyone how to live their life, or to point fingers at anyone, but instead to ask only the professed anti-government Christian voters and anti-government Christian politicians to please take another good look at your bible, so that you are reminded a little more of what calling yourself Christian should mean as a Christian politician or Christian voter. And if you as a professed Christian politician are going to refuse to do for the people what is right for them, according to God's word, by helping them instead of hurting them. Then many of us are asking you to stop dragging God's name into your dirty work of oppressive policy making.

From the beginning of this journey through our bibles, I set out with much prayer to prove to you beyond any doubt, that in using only bible scripture, the bible itself would prove to you far beyond any conservative argument, that God is absolutely positively in favor of nations whose governments help to eliminate poverty among all people while also helping all of the most in need among us, which you have seen that the early Christian church was such a terrific example of. And the early Christian church even went far beyond anything that I have suggested we should do as a nation. Because the early Christian church's governing of everyone's possessions was very possibly, the purest form of socialism that we could ever find. With over 200 bible scripture examples, God has shown you and I that these old conservative arguments against good governments for the benefit of all people, have now been very clearly and powerfully put to rest once and for all. The conservative Christian politician and conservative Christian voter cannot rightly argue any longer that a government which cares about its people is somehow too big, too bad or ungodly.

Even though these many bible scripture examples made all of the points for me with clear direction, I've still had to go way beyond my comfort zone in chapters 11 and 12 comparing it all to what it means today regarding America's 2 major political parties, the Democrats and the conservative Republican and Tea Party Republicans. Truth is what is important, and when we live by the truth, we have nothing to hide. Now that we have seen this very clear and powerful scriptural demonstration of things which are very politically relatable, which have also proven a multitude of times to be of extreme importance to God. We will now proceed with looking mainly at the 2 very political and controversial issues which keep the majority of today's American church voting for the conservative Republican oppressors of the American people. Both issues of which Jesus never talked about, abortions and gays.

CHAPTER THIRTEEN
Abortion Gay Marriage and Prayer in School

Our Political Choices in America Regarding Abortions and Gay Marriage.
More Liberal Democrats = A more prosperous majority.
Abortion and gay marriage are legal.
Conservative Republicans = Ever increasing oppression for the majority.
Abortion and Gay Marriage outlawed.

An abundance of bible scripture has proven to us over and over without question and far beyond any doubt, that those who read and believe their bible, should be very against anyone who oppresses people, especially anyone who oppresses the poor, needy and afflicted. This is by far the clearest and most absolute political message of the whole bible cover to cover. So Christians of all people should be by far, the most against those who oppress the people, second to none. The Christian church throughout the world should be highly concentrated on voting out the oppressors of the majority of the people, from positions of power and authority. And doing our best as God's people to keep the oppressors out of these positions of power and authority, always! No oppressors of the people in the governments of any nation, if we can possibly stop it, or prevent it. Yet mainly because of the issues of abortion and gay marriage, most of the American church votes for the scripturally proven oppressors of the vast majority of the people. The very oppressive conservative republicans, and the even more oppressive conservative Tea Party Republicans.

The issues of abortion and gay marriage are not the easiest things to talk about. But I will explain why I believe even as a Christian, that the far lesser of 2 evils is to keep abortion legal, and to allow gay couples to have the same legal rights as heterosexual couples that they deserve as people, and as citizens. This of course is a more liberal democratic government which would also immediately start to lessen all forms of oppression from the people until oppression would be eliminated. Oppression of all forms would finally be a thing of the past. And the future for all Americans would be much better in many ways. This would be a giant biblical step toward a truly Christian government in the elimination of oppression. But back to abortion and gay marriage. We will start with facing the historical reality of pre-Roe/Wade (when abortion was illegal) by asking you a very serious question.

Abortion Question For You

I don't believe that anyone likes abortion at all, but since making it illegal never even came close to stopping it, I believe this is a very appropriate question for all, especially for the most outspoken pro-lifers. What do you believe the punishment should be for a woman who has had an illegal abortion if it did become illegal again? Please think about this. You are the judge on the bench. What punishment would you hand to this (in many cases) very poor woman who has been convicted of having an illegal abortion? Please stop now and think about this for a moment. Take your time and really think about this for as long as it takes you to decide, before you continue reading.

I strongly believe that unless you have chosen to kill such a woman with capital punishment, you may actually be in favor of keeping abortion legal. You may actually be pro-choice. Here is the reality of why I say this.

Women have been attempting to have abortions for thousands of years, many dying in the process. Some say that abortion rates didn't go down very much even when it was illegal. In fact prior to the Roe/Wade decision in January of 1973 which made abortion legal, some say that abortion was actually the number one killer of women between the ages of 15 and 44 in America. So what is the major differences than, between keeping abortion legal in America as the Democrats desire to keep it, and what would it be like to turn the abortion clock back over 40 years, making abortion illegal again for women in America, like the conservative Republicans and conservative Tea Party Republicans desire to do?

The differences are huge regarding the woman's health. We must first consider our very young women who will often decide (without telling their parents) to have an abortion wherever they have to go. These are 14, 15, 16, 17 year old girls.

Here Are 2 Very Real Scenarios for You to Consider
Scenario #1

You have a 15 year old daughter who you love very much. She's been pretty quiet lately though and just acting different than normal. You've always had what you feel is a very good, positive relationship with her. You've asked her a few times lately if everything is alright and she insists that everything is, but you still sense that something isn't quite right with her.

Then one afternoon she doesn't show up home from school, and later that evening the police come to your door to tell you they found your precious daughter dead, and that she had bled to death from what appeared to be the result of a botched crude abortion.

You cry "she didn't tell me she was pregnant!"

This very abrupt kind of death was the outcome for thousands of families who had to lose their family members in these needless horrible painful miserable deaths from crude abortion practices, when abortion was illegal prior to the Roe/Wade decision in January of 1973 which allowed licensed practiced physicians to work on your children instead of the terrible brutal places that women and young girls used to go prior to Roe/Wade.

Many very good girls make mistakes. And many 14, 15, 16, 17, and 18 year olds are not going to tell their parents about their abortion plans. They will go where they can to get the abortion even when it's illegal, just exactly like they used to when they died in the procedure.

Should they be condemned to a horrible early death for this? And should everyone have to worry about their daughters again? Please think.

Scenario #2

Here is what happens today instead. Your 35 year old daughter who has been married for about 15 years and has 3 kids proceeds to tell you one day in shame that about 20 years ago she was pregnant and felt too unstable not only financially, but mentally also at that time to raise a child, plus she was in high school. So she made her mind up to have an abortion at the legal facility which had a staff of professional legal licensed doctors and nurses. You quickly realize that you are just grateful to God to have a healthy daughter, a healthy son in law, and 3 healthy grandchildren. Here is the result of abortion being safe and legal. Which scenario do you think is worse? Which one would you choose for a daughter you love?

Prohibiting alcohol never came close to stopping the consumption of alcohol, and prohibiting abortion never came close to stopping abortion. As for me, I realize that since making abortions illegal will never come close to stopping them, it will just mean that our very young 14, 15, 16, 17 year olds who are just kids and surely don't deserve to die, will just find where they can go to have the abortion which they have made up their minds already to have. This we will never be able to stop and history proves it. This is the reality of illegal abortion. But we do have some control. We can make sure that any woman who has an abortion will get it from a legal licensed doctor at a safe, clean sterile clinic, instead of a very scary place of God only knows. This much we can control. And historically we knew long ago that this was the far better way for the woman regarding this inevitable thing that's never going away.

So to me the far lesser of the 2 evils is to keep abortion legal since history has proven it's the far safer way, simply because abortions never stop when made illegal. They just become a huge threat to a woman's life when illegal, and many girls are never going to realize this. So the safety of the woman's health is what the importance of keeping abortion legal for women is about. The very obvious choice for a government which cares about its women is to keep abortion legal for the sake of that precious woman's life. For her future, and for her families best interest. To me this is an absolute no brainer. I wonder how many future children that all of the women would have had, that instead had to die very early needless extremely painful miserable deaths from botched layman so called "back alley abortions" when abortion was illegal prior to Roe/Wade. Republicans never talk about this reality that no woman should ever have to be forced to go back to. Remember, abortion won't stop, that's the reality of it. Because of that I conclude to remind you that we are supposed to love our neighbor as ourself. That's why under the inevitable circumstances of our world today, it is biblically more correct to leave the choice up to each woman, in what to do with her own body by keeping abortion legal for the lives of the woman to be saved.

God gave people free will, and love would let her decide for herself. I am not a fan of abortion, but for a society, if it's not legal, many women will die, and their future children will not have a chance to be born. I choose life for the pregnant woman, therefore I must choose that abortion stays legal.

Reviewing Politically What it Actually Means to the Woman

Democrats = pro-choice – your daughter lives.

Republicans = no choice – your daughter may die.

Pro-Life Should Mean Much More Than Pro-Birth

Republicans obviously don't call illegal abortion no-choice, they call it pro-life. But when you look at the Republican's views on everything as a whole, pro-life is just absolutely not a phrase that fits the Republican ideologies of legislating. Once a child is born to a very poor mother that woman and her child are completely on their own regardless of circumstances if the Republicans have their way in the matter. Republicans are completely against helping that mother if she needs help. Republicans have vehemently tried to repeal the affordable healthcare for America act 40 times! Republicans don't care if that baby has a major health problem, they have proven it 40 times and they are not finished trying yet.

Their problem currently is that there is just barely enough Democrats in congress to keep the Republicans from being able to take these things away from the families. Shouldn't those who seem to be so concerned about the lives of the unborn be equally concerned about the lives of the recently born? These so called pro-life Republicans don't want to give an extremely poor mother food stamps to feed that baby, or anything else once it's born. No temporary assistance if it's a needy family, no day care, no head start, no early childhood education or children's healthcare. Republican governors are even cutting child protection workers who handle child abuse and neglect cases. Republicans are cutting as many services for the people as they possibly can, in order to give it all back only to the corporate rich in even more tax breaks. Republicans don't want to hear anything about that kid once it's born. That's absolutely not pro-life.

If republicans were really concerned about reducing the amount of abortions, they could start by raising the minimum wage up to a livable wage for people with children. This they will probably never do unless yet another huge tax break for the wealthy is attached to the minimum wage bill. Raising the minimum wage alone would lessen the abortion rates in America. What about increasing contraception coverage? Republicans are against this as well, but it surely would reduce the abortion rate. What about more childhood education about how early pregnancies will surely change your child's plans? Again Republicans are always against anything that cost money because this would mean that we just might have to raise taxes on the wealthiest Americans including the Republican guarded corporations enough again to help with these real situations that seriously need our attention. Republicans who are against these things that would greatly reduce the number of abortions, and are also very demanding of what would make abortion very dangerous again for the mother, in my opinion have absolutely no right to call themselves pro-life.

Republicans, why if you are pro-life, are you also pro-war, pro-torture, pro-assault weapons in the hands of all, pro-death penalty, pro-nuclear weapons, pro-anti-environment against the protection of our air, water and soul? Why do you pro-life Republicans take away food stamps and fuel assistance from the poor? Why if you're pro-life are you trying to make voting so difficult for many? Is this really your idea of being pro-life? Really? Why if you're pro-life do you seem to insist that America must spend more on defense for more wars than the next 10 highest spending countries war spending combined? Yet you are so violently against affordable healthcare for all that you have tried to take away from us all 40 times so far, what is only the weak beginnings of more affordable healthcare for all.

Why why why if you are pro-life can't America only spend as much on war as maybe only the next 7 highest countries war spending combined instead of 10 countries combined war spending? Then every American could have free healthcare including prescriptions. But I guess you Republicans are just too pro-life to care about saving your own people from sickness. So in light of these few truths plus many others not mentioned, I cannot agree with my fellow church goers in their voting for the very oppressive Republican party as they call the Republicans pro-life. I believe much more realistically that the Republicans are actually much more pro-against taxing the wealthy for anything that would help all of America's people with even the most basic of needs which we have proven biblically to be the basics of Christianity.

Democrats on the other hand are for helping the people from the baby to its mother to the most elderly among us which has been proven to us to be much more biblically correct. But the wealthy must be taxed at higher rates of old for many conditions to be right again. When you add everything up regarding the differences between the Democrats and Republicans, there is no question that the Democrats are much more the closest party in America politically to the teachings of the bible by rightly helping the people. Including saving the life of the young woman who is going to have an abortion, legal or not. Because ending Roe/Wade is not about stopping abortions. History has proven that will never even come close to happening. Keeping Roe/Wade is about saving the many women's lives when they have that inevitable abortion.

Sure abortion is an ugly subject. But since it never stops in a society, legalized abortion will keep the woman safe, alive and keep the families together. That's why I believe today that in loving my neighbor as myself. Abortion that doesn't kill the woman is much more on the side of loving my neighbor as myself, than abortion that's illegal, which does kill many women. That's why I also will take any bible scripture that you may say supports the fetus, in even higher regard to saving the mother's life, and doing so by supporting keeping abortions safe, by keeping it legal.

Gay Marriage

I am straight and never married, but throughout my life I have learned that several really good people whom I have met and known, just happen to be gay. Few of the most fortunate ones are in a happy committed relationship with someone who really loves them, and I think that's great. I don't think that anything this world has to offer is worth much, compared to what it must be like, to be in a happy committed relationship with someone who you love very much, who also feels the same about you. This to me is truly a gift from God. I have learned a few very important things from asking these friends about their lives as gay people. I have learned that they knew they were different at a very young age, like less than 10 years old. I have learned that they would have given almost anything to not be gay, and to be attracted to the opposite sex. So this was not a choice for them that they just chose to make one day. This was not just a gay lifestyle that they chose to make, this was not a choice for them. So life for these people is not easy.

I do not view any of these good people any differently than I view anyone else. They are good responsible individuals who I am happy are a part of the community in which I live. I would help them as much as I would help anyone else for the sake of what is right for them. Why shouldn't I? I have tried to imagine how much more difficult their lives must be, and I have no idea I'm sure. I have no doubt that my gay friends who are couples love each other just as much as anyone could love another human being. Not that my opinion matters about this because it shouldn't. I believe there are gay couples who probably love each other more than many heterosexual couples, some of which are worried about gay marriage violating the sanctity of their 2nd, 3rd, or 4th marriage. This gay marriage issue seems mostly about gays having equal legal rights in their relationship.

Don't you think that when two people are in a committed relationship together for a lifetime, that it's really about a whole lot more than just sex? Of course it is! Love is much more than sex, its total commitment.

What if you were with your loving lifelong partner for about 20 years or more? And he or she suddenly had to be taken one day by ambulance only to find out that he or she was terminally ill and didn't have long to live. But you suddenly find out that you cannot visit your loved one in the hospital because you are not considered a family member. Crucial decisions had to be made for your loved one but you were not able to make them. Your partner dies and you also have no inheritance rights. This would not make any logical sense at all. Not long ago there were stories like these happening. Some progress has been made for this human rights issue but the gay marriage issue is all about rights that gays should not be denied. There are several legal rights that we heterosexuals take for granted that gay couples have been denied that add up to big things. Joint tax filing rights, employee coinsurance rights and inheritance rights such as Social Security for example. Why should gay couples be treated like second class citizens? Do you really believe as a Christian that this is loving your neighbor as yourself? Republicans have no problem denying equal rights to gays, women and minorities. Democrats believe that gay couples deserve the same legal rights as heterosexual couples. Let's look again at Jesus greatest commandment of all, to love our neighbor as ourself. How do your decisions line up here?

Matthew 22:34-40 (NASB)

[34] But when the Pharisees heard that Jesus had silenced the Sadducees, they gathered themselves together. [35] One of them, a lawyer, asked Him a question, testing Him, [36] "Teacher, which is the great commandment in the Law?" [37] And He said to him, "'YOU SHALL LOVE THE LORD YOUR GOD WITH ALL YOUR HEART, AND WITH ALL YOUR SOUL, AND WITH ALL YOUR

MIND.' [38] This is the great and foremost commandment. [39] The second is like it, 'YOU SHALL LOVE YOUR NEIGHBOR AS YOURSELF.' [40] On these two commandments depend the whole Law and the Prophets."

Now in light of part of Jesus most important commandment in loving our neighbor as ourself, who do you believe the gay couples in America would say loves them? The Democrats who want to legislate what is fair for them in giving them equal rights, or the Republicans who desire to keep them bound to no choices once again, and without equal rights? Who would you say is loving you if you were the gay couple, the Democrats or the Republicans? Remember once again that Jesus said in this last example from Matthew 22 to love the Lord your God with all your heart, soul and mind. He calls this the great and foremost commandment, but then says the second is like it. The second being that you shall love your neighbor as yourself. But how Jesus finishes this is what really makes this the most important commandment when He says "On these two commandments depend the whole law and the prophets." The whole law, all of it!

So I ask the politicians who want us to know they are Christian and I also ask the Christian voters. If we are calling ourselves Christians, shouldn't this mean that we should be holding Christ words to the highest regard of the whole bible? Christ, Christian? Remember Jesus giving us 7 examples of the importance of His words in Chapter One? But what about the Old Testament and all of the laws of God? It surely hasn't lost its importance, in fact it is extremely relevant to us all, and it convicts every single one of us as sinners. Everyone is guilty according to the law, everyone! We are all so much as equalized by the Old Testament in needing this most important thing in the bible called God's grace and mercy. Which of course is only attained biblically from our faith in the sacrifice that Jesus made for us all in His perfect life, death, and resurrection.

So if we want to pick and choose the sins which we believe are worse than our own, we have an immediate losing battle against the word of God, because according to our bibles, everyone is guilty of sin, and just as in need as anyone else. Except those who reject Christ, in whose case biblically is no hope.

Psalm 14:1-3 (NASB)
Folly and Wickedness of Men.
For the choir director. A Psalm of David.
[1] The fool has said in his heart, "There is no God."
They are corrupt, they have committed
abominable deeds;
There is no one who does good.
[2] The Lord has looked down from heaven upon the
sons of men
To see if there are any who understand,
Who seek after God.
[3] They have all turned aside, together they have
become corrupt;
There is no one who does good, not even one.

James 2:8-13 (NASB)
[8] If, however, you are fulfilling the royal law
according to the Scripture, "You shall love your
neighbor as yourself," you are doing well. [9] But if
you show partiality, you are committing sin and are
convicted by the law as transgressors. [10] For
whoever keeps the whole law and yet stumbles in
one point, he has become guilty of all. [11] For He
who said, "Do not commit adultery," also said, "Do
not commit murder." Now if you do not commit
adultery, but do commit murder, you have become a
transgressor of the law. [12] So speak and so act as
those who are to be judged by the law of

liberty. ¹³ For judgment will be merciless to one who
has shown no mercy; mercy triumphs over
judgment.

Look at verse 10. You could keep the whole law and stumble at only one point and you become guilty of all. As Christians we should all know that the law was intended for such purpose, to convict everyone as a sinner. And even the smallest sin in our eyes convicts us as breaking the whole law. So we shouldn't try and think we are better than anyone else. Look at verse 13. For judgment will be merciless to one who has shown no mercy; mercy triumphs over judgment.

Romans 3:10 (NASB)
¹⁰ as it is written,
"There is none righteous, not even one

Romans 3:23 (NASB)
²³ for all have sinned and fall short of the glory of
God

James 4:17 (NASB)
¹⁷ Therefore, to one who knows the right thing to do
and does not do it, to him it is sin.

Even if you know the right thing that you should do, and you just decide not to do it, this convicts you essentially of breaking the whole law! Look at the last 2 scripture examples. If this is boring to you, please hang in there while we all get on the same page as being guilty of being sinners. So we must be saved from our sins and as Christians we have learned that this only comes through our faith in Christ and what He did for us. And we need to put all of our faith in God's grace through Christ Jesus. Because all of our lives are full of mistakes, all of us whether we admit it or not. Is the church today preaching more law or grace?

More old testament or new? Is the church inviting to and attracting gay people? Do gay people feel a hope and desire to go to your church because it preaches God's grace? Salvation of the souls is what is important to us Christians right? Then are we inviting people or pushing them away with our words and actions? Yes every one of us is just as guilty as the next person according to the standards of the laws of God. But we are all justified by God's grace through our faith in Christ Jesus.

Romans 6:23 (NASB)

[23] For the wages of sin is death, but the free gift of God is eternal life in Christ Jesus our Lord

Romans 5:8 (NASB)

[8] But God demonstrates His own love toward us, in that while we were yet sinners, Christ died for us.

Titus 3:5 (NASB)

[5] He saved us, not on the basis of deeds which we have done in righteousness, but according to His mercy, by the washing of regeneration and renewing by the Holy Spirit,

Romans 3:19-28 (NASB)

[19] Now we know that whatever the Law says, it speaks to those who are under the Law, so that every mouth may be closed and all the world may become accountable to God; [20] because by the works of the Law no flesh will be justified in His sight; for through the Law comes the knowledge of sin.

Justification by Faith

²¹ But now apart from the Law the righteousness of God has been manifested, being witnessed by the Law and the Prophets, ²² even the righteousness of God through faith in Jesus Christ for all those who believe; for there is no distinction; ²³ for all have sinned and fall short of the glory of God, ²⁴ being justified as a gift by His grace through the redemption which is in Christ Jesus; ²⁵ whom God displayed publicly as a propitiation in His blood through faith. This was to demonstrate His righteousness, because in the forbearance of God He passed over the sins previously committed; ²⁶ for the demonstration, I say, of His righteousness at the present time, so that He would be just and the justifier of the one who has faith in Jesus.
²⁷ Where then is boasting? It is excluded. By what kind of law? Of works? No, but by a law of faith. ²⁸ For we maintain that a man is justified by faith apart from works of the Law.

Galatians 3 (NASB)
Faith Brings Righteousness

¹ You foolish Galatians, who has bewitched you, before whose eyes Jesus Christ was publicly portrayed as crucified? ² This is the only thing I want to find out from you: did you receive the Spirit by the works of the Law, or by hearing with faith? ³ Are you so foolish? Having begun by the Spirit, are you now being perfected by the flesh? ⁴ Did you suffer so many things in vain—if

indeed it was in vain? [5] So then, does He
who provides you with the Spirit and works
miracles among you, do it by the works of the Law,
or by hearing with faith?
[6] Even so Abraham believed God, and it was
reckoned to him as righteousness. [7] Therefore, be
sure that it is those who are of faith who are sons of
Abraham. [8] The Scripture, foreseeing that
God would justify the Gentiles by faith, preached
the gospel beforehand to Abraham, saying, "All the
nations will be blessed in you." [9] So then those who
are of faith are blessed with Abraham, the believer.
[10] For as many as are of the works of the Law are
under a curse; for it is written, "Cursed is everyone
who does not abide by all things written in the book
of the law, to perform them." [11] Now that no one is
justified by the Law before God is evident; for,
"The righteous man shall live by faith." [12] However,
the Law is not of faith; on the contrary, "He who
practices them shall live by
them." [13] Christ redeemed us from the curse of the
Law, having become a curse for us—for it is
written, "Cursed is everyone who hangs
on a tree"— [14] in order that in Christ Jesus the
blessing of Abraham might come to the Gentiles, so
that we would receive the promise of the Spirit
through faith.

Intent of the Law

[15] Brethren, I speak in terms of human
relations: even though it is only a man's covenant,

yet when it has been ratified, no one sets it aside or adds conditions to it. [16] Now the promises were spoken to Abraham and to his seed. He does not say, "And to seeds," as referring to many, but rather to one, "And to your seed," that is, Christ. [17] What I am saying is this: the Law, which came four hundred and thirty years later, does not invalidate a covenant previously ratified by God, so as to nullify the promise. [18] For if the inheritance is based on law, it is no longer based on a promise; but God has granted it to Abraham by means of a promise. [19] Why the Law then? It was added because of transgressions, having been ordained through angels by the agency of a mediator, until the seed would come to whom the promise had been made. [20] Now a mediator is not for one party only; whereas God is only one. [21] Is the Law then contrary to the promises of God? May it never be! For if a law had been given which was able to impart life, then righteousness would indeed have been based on law. [22] But the Scripture has shut up everyone under sin, so that the promise by faith in Jesus Christ might be given to those who believe. [23] But before faith came, we were kept in custody under the law, being shut up to the faith which was later to be revealed. [24] Therefore the Law has become our tutor to lead us to Christ, so that we may be justified by faith. [25] But now that faith has come, we are no longer under a tutor. [26] For you are all sons of God through faith in Christ Jesus.[27] For all of you who were baptized into Christ have clothed yourselves with Christ. [28] There is neither Jew nor Greek, there is neither slave nor free man, there is neither male nor female; for you are all one in Christ Jesus. ²⁹ And if you belong to Christ, then you are Abraham's descendants, heirs according to promise.

Luke 18:9-14 (NASB)
The Pharisee and the Publican

⁹ And He also told this parable to some people who trusted in themselves that they were righteous, and viewed others with contempt: ¹⁰ "Two men went up into the temple to pray, one a Pharisee and the other a tax collector. ¹¹ The Pharisee stood and was praying this to himself: 'God, I thank You that I am not like other people: swindlers, unjust, adulterers, or even like this tax collector. ¹² I fast twice a week; I pay tithes of all that I get.' ¹³ But the tax collector, standing some distance away, was even unwilling to lift up his eyes to heaven, but was beating his breast, saying, 'God, be merciful to me, the sinner!' ¹⁴ I tell you, this man went to his house justified rather than the other; for everyone who exalts himself will be humbled, but he who humbles himself will be exalted."

So our faith, our belief, is most important, because we all miss it somewhere a million times at least, especially if our wrongful thoughts are considered.

Matthew 21:28-32 (NASB)
Parable of Two Sons

²⁸ "But what do you think? A man had two sons, and he came to the first and said, 'Son, go work today in

the vineyard.'²⁹ And he answered, 'I will not'; but afterward he regretted it and went. ³⁰ The man came to the second and said the same thing; and he answered, 'I will, sir'; but he did not go. ³¹ Which of the two did the will of his father?" They said, "The first." Jesus said to them, "Truly I say to you that the tax collectors and prostitutes will get into the kingdom of God before you. ³² For John came to you in the way of righteousness and you did not believe him; but the tax collectors and prostitutes did believe him; and you, seeing this, did not even feel remorse afterward so as to believe him."

Jesus was speaking there in Matthew 21 of John the Baptist, who God sent ahead of Jesus to prepare the way for Him. But how much more biblically important it is to believe in Jesus words for salvation. Straight or gay has absolutely nothing to do with any of it. Notice in verse 31 Jesus mentions the possibility of prostitutes getting into the Kingdom of God, before this group of people who thought they were righteous.

John 3:17-21 (NASB)

¹⁷ For God did not send the Son into the world to judge the world, but that the world might be saved through Him.¹⁸ He who believes in Him is not judged; he who does not believe has been judged already, because he has not believed in the name of the only begotten Son of God. ¹⁹ This is the judgment, that the Light has come into the world, and men loved the darkness rather than the Light, for their deeds were evil. ²⁰ For everyone who does

evil hates the Light, and does not come to the Light for fear that his deeds will be exposed. **21** But he who practices the truth comes to the Light, so that his deeds may be manifested as having been wrought in God."

Mark 2:14-17 (NASB)
Levi (Matthew) Called

14 As He passed by, He saw Levi the son of Alphaeus sitting in the tax booth, and He *said to him, "Follow Me!" And he got up and followed Him.

15 And it *happened that He was reclining at the table in his house, and many tax collectors and sinners were dining with Jesus and His disciples; for there were many of them, and they were following Him. **16** When the scribes of the Pharisees saw that He was eating with the sinners and tax collectors, they said to His disciples, "Why is He eating and drinking with tax collectors and sinners?" **17** And hearing this, Jesus *said to them, "It is not those who are healthy who need a physician, but those who are sick; I did not come to call the righteous, but sinners."

Psalm 145:8-9 (NASB)

8 The Lord is gracious and merciful;
Slow to anger and great in lovingkindness.
9 The Lord is good to all,
And His mercies are over all His works.

John 6:47 (KJV)

[47]"Verily, verily, I say unto you, He that believeth on me hath everlasting life."

John 3:16 (NASB)

[16] "For God so loved the world, that He gave His only begotten Son, that whoever believes in Him shall not perish, but have eternal life."

Ephesians 2:8-9 (NASB)

[8] For by grace you have been saved through faith; and that not of yourselves, it is the gift of God; [9] not as a result of works, so that no one may boast.

Salvation of everyone is most important to God. And it comes by faith, not works. Have you considered Jesus for your salvation? Is your name written in the Lamb's Book of Life?

Romans 10:9-13 (NASB)

[9] that if you confess with your mouth Jesus as Lord, and believe in your heart that God raised Him from the dead, you will be saved; [10] for with the heart a person believes, resulting in righteousness, and with the mouth he confesses, resulting in salvation. [11] For the Scripture says, "WHOEVER BELIEVES IN HIM WILL NOT BE DISAPPOINTED." [12] For there is no distinction between Jew and Greek; for the same Lord is Lord of all, abounding in riches for all who call on Him; [13] for "WHOEVER WILL CALL ON THE NAME OF THE LORD WILL BE SAVED."

So I will never try to stop 2 people who love each other from uniting together. And if they know of a church that will marry them I think that's great. In America our people think nothing of sending these 2 gay people to war to kill, be killed or maimed for life. And if they kill enough people in the right situation, they just may receive great honor for this. Yet if these same 2 gay people truly love each other and want to give all of themselves to each other in a lifelong commitment of love, America's church says absolutely not, we can't have that.

This somehow doesn't seem right to me biblically. Especially when I consider the sexual lives of some of the patriarchs of the bible whom I believe most church goers look up to. Abraham for example had more than one wife as did Jacob also. King David had at least 8 wives and 10 concubines. And if we look at King David's path to marrying Solomon's mother Bathsheba, this we would have to admit was far less than what we could call a righteous union. Yet most Christians in America sing psalms written by King David every week in church. David's son Solomon had 700 wives and 300 concubines. So biblically at least in the Old Testament, marriage between one man and one woman is not so prevalent. God even called David a man after my own heart. David's heart was right with God despite David's weakness in the flesh. Should we really continue to deny giving equal rights to gay couples? I believe we should give them equal rights and instead try to continuously better ourselves, for the sake of others according to Jesus words.

Matthew 7:1-5 (NASB)
Judging Others

[1] "Do not judge so that you will not be judged. [2] For in the way you judge, you will be judged; and by your standard of measure, it will be measured to you. [3] Why do you look at the speck that is in your brother's eye, but do not notice the log that is in your own eye? [4] Or how can you say to your brother, 'Let me take the speck out of your eye,' and behold, the log is in your own eye? [5] You

hypocrite, first take the log out of your own eye, and then you will see clearly to take the speck out of your brother's eye.

John 8:1-11 (NASB)
The Adulterous Woman

[1] But Jesus went to the Mount of Olives. [2] Early in the morning He came again into the temple, and all the people were coming to Him; and He sat down and began to teach them. [3] The scribes and the Pharisees brought a woman caught in adultery, and having set her in the center of the court, [4] they said to Him, "Teacher, this woman has been caught in adultery, in the very act. [5] Now in the Law Moses commanded us to stone such women; what then do You say?" [6] They were saying this, testing Him, so that they might have grounds for accusing Him. But Jesus stooped down and with His finger wrote on the ground. [7] But when they persisted in asking Him, He straightened up, and said to them, "He who is without sin among you, let him be the first to throw a stone at her." [8] Again He stooped down and wrote on the ground. [9] When they heard it, they began to go out one by one, beginning with the older ones, and He was left alone, and the woman, where she was, in the center of the court. [10] Straightening up, Jesus said to her, "Woman, where are they? Did no one condemn you?" [11] She said, "No one, Lord." And Jesus said, "I do not condemn you, either. Go. From now on sin no more."

Do you think Jesus answer would have been any different to the accusers if they had dragged a couple of gay people to Him who were caught in the act? Or if they had dragged a woman who had been caught in the act of trying to self-abort a pregnancy? I don't believe Jesus answer would have been any different no matter what the sin had been. So it's not right for a Christian to pick and choose which sins we think are worse than the ones we have been guilty of because biblically, sin is sin and all are guilty. That's why I am not even going to list the biblical examples written out which are against homosexual relationships because if I bring out some of the law, then I must also bring out all of the law in the conviction of literally everyone as guilty sinners. But only because we are on the subject of gay marriage, I will list out where you can find the scriptural examples in regard to homosexual relations if you choose to look them up. But once again, if I throw stones at gay people or women who have had abortions, I should immediately realize that according to the laws of God, I am also just as guilty of sin in some way as the one whom I accuse.

Scripture List
Leviticus 18:22
Leviticus 20:13
Romans 1:26-32
1 Corinthians 6:9-11
1 Timothy 1:8-10

So what is left for us to consider at the end of the matter? To love one another as ourselves. And we can't rightly do this without really considering what it's like to be in their shoes. Maybe the church could at least agree to giving gay couples the equal rights they deserve in civil unions without calling it marriage, if nothing else. The church surely isn't loving these people as Jesus told us to until we agree to give them the equal legal rights which they deserve. So by the Old Testament laws all of us are convicted as sinners. And by the new testament all of us are acquitted by God's grace through our faith in Christ Jesus.

Therefore to recap, the bottom line of the issues of abortion and gay marriage. No matter how much we hate abortion, it will always be happening in really big numbers even if made illegal again. But multitudes of women will die needless, miserable deaths like times past when abortion was illegal, if made illegal again. So the abortion issue in America today is not about us successfully stopping abortions from happening. This can't be done no matter how illegal abortion becomes, history proves it. So the abortion issue is all about saving the women's lives who have abortions. Keeping abortion legal by supporting Roe/Wade saves the lives of multitudes of women. The gay marriage issue is not about removing gay people from society. Gay people will always continue to live their lives. The gay marriage issue is simply about giving gay couples who love and care about each other the same legal rights as heterosexual couples. When all of the hype is removed from these 2 issues, the reality is that simple. Love helps people to live better lives.

1 Peter 4:8 (NASB)
[8] Above all, keep fervent in your love for one
another, because love covers a multitude of sins.

Romans 13:8-10 (NASB)
[8] Owe nothing to anyone except to love one another;
for he who loves his neighbor has
fulfilled the law. [9] For this, "You shall not commit
adultery, You shall not murder, You shall not steal,
You shall not covet," and if there is any other
commandment, it is summed up in this saying, "You
shall love your neighbor as yourself." [10] Love does
no wrong to a neighbor; therefore love is the
fulfillment of the law.
1 Corinthians 13 (NASB)
The Excellence of Love
[1] If I speak with the tongues of men and of angels,

but do not have love, I have become a noisy gong or a clanging cymbal. [2] If I have the gift of prophecy, and know all mysteries and all knowledge; and if I have all faith, so as to remove mountains, but do not have love, I am nothing. [3] And if I give all my possessions to feed the poor, and if I surrender my body to be burned, but do not have love, it profits me nothing. [4] Love is patient, love is kind and is not jealous; love does not brag and is not arrogant, [5] does not act unbecomingly; it does not seek its own, is not provoked, does not take into account a wrong suffered, [6] does not rejoice in unrighteousness, but rejoices with the truth; [7] bears all things, believes all things, hopes all things, endures all things.

[8] Love never fails; but if there are gifts of prophecy, they will be done away; if there are tongues, they will cease; if there is knowledge, it will be done away. [9] For we know in part and we prophesy in part; [10] but when the perfect comes, the partial will be done away. [11] When I was a child, I used to speak like a child, think like a child, reason like a child; when I became a man, I did away with childish things. [12] For now we see in a mirror dimly, but then face to face; now I know in part, but then I will know fully just as I also have been fully known. [13] But now faith, hope, love, abide these three; but the greatest of these is love.

Prayer in School

Here is something which Jesus said that I believe my fellow Christian's should consider about this subject.

Matthew 6:5-8 (NASB)

[5] "When you pray, you are not to be like the hypocrites; for they love to stand and pray in the synagogues and on the street corners so that they may be seen by men. Truly I say to you, they have their reward in full. [6] But you, when you pray, go into your inner room, close your door and pray to your Father who is in secret, and your Father who sees what is done in secret will reward you. [7] "And when you are praying, do not use meaningless repetition as the Gentiles do, for they suppose that they will be heard for their many words. [8] So do not be like them; for your Father knows what you need before you ask Him.

Because of the simple fact that Jesus was very specific about the subject of prayer, as a Christian, I must consider the political subject of prayer in school as a non-issue. As you can see in verse 6 of Matthew 6, Jesus directs us to be very private about our praying. I have lived some amazing results of prayer and if I had children, I would teach them of the absolute value of prayer. And that they are always able to pray in their thoughts to God at anytime, anyplace. I do believe in equal rights in the classroom on the issues of creationism and evolution. To me in full fairness, both should be given equal time in the classroom if either are in the plans of mentioning, in order to keep as much peace as possible among all people. If this gets complicated and can't be done, then perhaps neither should be taught in the classroom.

Refocusing on the 2 Issues Which Jesus Never Talked About, Abortion and Gay Marriage.

Since everyone must accept the fact that gay couples will continue to exist in this world. If you believe it's evil to give them equal rights in allowing them to unite legally, I then must ask you to consider which of these choices are worse for a nation's people, when made legal by the laws of a nation. Especially when we consider that the early church shared everything to eliminate the needs of all. No needy were found among them.

Which is Worse for a Nation's People When Made Legal?

1. Millionaires, billionaires, and churches not having to pay tax into the government to help with all of the needs of the people.
2. Our nation spending more on defense for more war than the next 10 highest war spending countries combined.
3. Keeping abortion safe by keeping it legal since it never stops when made illegal, yet kills many women when its illegal.
4. Legalized gay marriage allowing full legal married rights for gay couples.

If you believe that 3 and 4 are worse for a nation than 1 and 2, then you must somehow completely disregard nearly all of the scripture examples which you have just read in *Bible Politics* concerning a nation's people. Especially the poor, needy, hungry, helpless, orphan, afflicted, widow, fatherless, alien (immigrant) stranger and all who are oppressed. In today's world of high populations, the governments of the nations must be built to consider this huge group of people (the masses) which at some point in time involves literally every family in every nation. We have been proven over and over scripturally that the more liberal governments such as the Democrats which attempt to eliminate at least the basic needs of the people are far more in line with scripture than the conservative governments such as the Republican, Tea Party and Libertarian parties which ignore the needs of the people only to satisfy the desires of the corporations and the super-rich. These conservative political parties are doing just the opposite of what a government's focus should be, at least if you are trying to attach Christianity to it.

Remember, Jesus will put Himself in the shoes of those who are most in need as He will speak to the Nations, which are the very people whom the conservative political parties bluntly reject and oppress. I find that it's much easier to defend the Democrats with a bible who defend 3 and 4 than it is to defend the conservative Republican and Tea Party who defend 1 and 2. Here is another look at Jesus in Matthew chapter 25.

Matthew 25:31-46 (NASB)
The Judgment

[31] "But when the Son of Man comes in His glory, and all the angels with Him, then He will sit on His glorious throne. [32] All the nations will be gathered before Him; and He will separate them from one another, as the shepherd separates the sheep from the goats; [33] and He will put the sheep on His right, and the goats on the left.

[34] "Then the King will say to those on His right, 'Come, you who are blessed of My Father, inherit the kingdom prepared for you from the foundation of the world. [35] For I was hungry, and you gave Me something to eat; I was thirsty, and you gave Me something to drink; I was a stranger, and you invited Me in; [36] naked, and you clothed Me; I was sick, and you visited Me; I was in prison, and you came to Me.' [37] Then the righteous will answer Him, 'Lord, when did we see You hungry, and feed You, or thirsty, and give You something to drink? [38] And when did we see You a stranger, and invite You in, or naked, and clothe You? [39] When did we see You sick, or in prison, and come to You?' [40] The King will answer and say to them, 'Truly I say to you, to the extent that you did it to one of these brothers of

Mine, even the least of them, you did it to Me.'
[41] "Then He will also say to those on His left,
'Depart from Me, accursed ones, into the eternal
fire which has been prepared for the devil and his
angels; [42] for I was hungry, and you gave
Me nothing to eat; I was thirsty, and you gave Me
nothing to drink; [43] I was a stranger, and you did not
invite Me in; naked, and you did not clothe Me;
sick, and in prison, and you did not visit
Me.' [44] Then they themselves also will answer,
'Lord, when did we see You hungry, or thirsty, or a
stranger, or naked, or sick, or in prison, and did
not take care of You?' [45] Then He will answer them,
'Truly I say to you, to the extent that you did not do
it to one of the least of these, you did not do it to
Me.' [46] These will go away into eternal punishment,
but the righteous into eternal life."

CHAPTER FOURTEEN
Our Political Choices Determine Who We Are Serving as Politicians and Voters

Matthew 6:24 (NASB)
[24] "No one can serve two masters; for either he will hate the one and love the other, or he will be devoted to one and despise the other. You cannot serve God and wealth.

We Vote For Our Government to Either Serve We the People or For Our Government to Serve Corporations Instead

Focusing one last time on Jesus words from Matthew 6:24 because it is the foundation of the heart of nearly every political issue. Please take a good look at it again. Let's not forget that a huge part of loving God is loving people. So again, are our political decisions serving and loving people more or money? People, or corporations? That is the question.

Scripture has overwhelmingly proven to us that God is much more in favor and approving of the governments of nations, whose primary goal is about the betterment of the lives of all its people, not just the very wealthy. And attempting to eliminate at very least the basic needs of all people, as was in the early church, whose leaders were taught by Jesus Himself. So we have seen here and conclude that a government which is most correct with the bible, is one that is fair and promotes justice for all people, a government which attempts to eliminate inequality of opportunity.

Remember John the Baptist? Here is something John the Baptist said which obviously represents true biblical Christianity, since God sent John to prepare the way for Jesus.

Luke 3:11 (NASB)

[11] And he would answer and say to them, "The man who has two tunics is to share with him who has none; and he who has food is to do likewise."

What does the teaching of today's corporate conservative Republican Christianity call this kind of teaching? Socialism! This scripture alone strongly supports the nations' governments whose goal is to eliminate inequality of opportunity collectively together as a people. I personally don't believe you can say that you believe in biblical Christianity, and also hold to the teachings of conservative Christianity. You must let one or the other go.

I didn't write *Bible Politics* to try and tell anyone how to live their lives. My main purpose was first toward the professed Christian politicians. To prove to them that they should be concentrated on working for the people and not for the corporations, if they are eager to mention their Christianity to all of us. If they are going to work against the needs of the people in order to do the desires of the corporations, my hope is that they would consider not reminding us of their Christianity. Since they have now been proven that selling out the people for the corporations is not a Christian value. And regarding my Christian voting friends. We have learned that being against good government services such as Social Security, Medicare, Medicaid and the Patient Protection and Affordable Care Act "Obamacare" is actually very much against Christian values since every one of these government services helps millions of people to live better lives. So we need to be in favor of these good government services. We have also learned not to be against immigration because that is simply against Christian values. We have learned not to be against the people who are trying to protect our air, water, and soil from unnecessary pollution. We should be on their side, not against them. We have learned that there were no needy people in the early Church and if our government took lessons from the early church we wouldn't have any needy people in our society today. We have also learned that in those times of not having any needy people among them there were also no corporations getting in the way of the peoples' needs, because there simply were no corporations.

Contrary to most of my fellow American Christians today, here is what I believe is actually the most ungodly problem with America's government today. The following quote from Bernie Sanders (I) Vermont Senator was lightly mentioned in Chapter 12 already. Recently the Republicans called just the thought of raising taxes on people like millionaires and billionaires (owners of big corporations) "class warfare." Here is what one of my favorite Senators from Vermont (an Independent) Bernie Sanders had to say about the Republicans "class warfare" comment. Bernie said "They talk about class-warfare- the fact of the matter is there has been class warfare for the last 30 years" he said on MSNBC's *Politics Nation*. "It's a handful of billionaires taking on the entire middle-class and working-class of this country." "And the result is, you now have in America the most unequal distribution of wealth and income of any major country on earth and the worst inequality in America since 1928." "How could anybody defend the top 400 richest people in this country owning more wealth than the bottom half of America, 150 million people?"

They Are Just Getting Started

This is only the beginning of the total collapse of America's middle class and vast majority. Make no mistake about it, these billionaires are coming for your Social Security and Medicare, along with the poor and disabled people's Medicaid just for starters all in the name of privatization. As I write, the Republicans are threatening to shut down America's government simply to defund the Patient Protection and Affordable Care Act also known as "Obamacare." The Republicans in the House have now tried 40 times to repeal the Patient Protection and Affordable Care Act as was already mentioned.

The Republicans have also been working hard on shutting down our wonderful and efficient United States Postal Service since 2006. Our postal service has always been the most reasonable and reliable way to send just about anything. It is more than competitive with the other postal services and also hasn't taken a single tax dollar to operate. Our United States Post Office pays all of its expenses on just the services which it sells, mainly the sale of stamps. Again our post office hasn't used any tax dollars whatsoever. But the Republican corporate businessmen want to shut down our postal system to put it into the hands of private owners. So in 2006 they passed a law that would suddenly require our now 238 year old time tested wonderfully cheap post office to come up with 75 years of future pensions for its employees in only 10 years. That's even for employees who are not even born yet! This is truly a manufactured crisis. And so far, it looks like the Republicans are going to get away with this. How much will a stamp cost us once their private for profit corporation takes over our once wonderful postal system? Well this is just the start of what these for profit corporate businessmen who go into politics want to do with everything that is government related. Even police and fire protection will be in addition to your tax dollars someday if these corporate Republicans have their way. When these corporate politicians tell us how bad government is and that the private sector can do everything better this is what is really on their minds.

This is obviously not *Bible Politics*. This is nothing other than corporate driven politics against the vast majority of the people. The Republicans have also come after our unions in their attempts to destroy the working person's voice and ability to collectively bargain. And this after they took over the House of Representatives in 2010 promising job creation; Remember? They have since voted against all of the president's jobs bills. If these corporate Republicans are successful in destroying America's unions the effects of it will immediately start to sweep across our nation. Soon after there will be no more minimum wage, no more 40 hour work week, no more overtime after 40, no more vacation days or sick days. And no more retirement benefits at work. And once the corporations have successfully taken all of these things from the Average American mostly through the corporate Republican Party, and once they have also been successful in taking away our Social Security, Medicare, and Medicaid, most Americans will have to work till the day they die.

The Republicans truly are working for those 400 wealthiest people and their corporations instead of us 317 million people. And so are any of these small government is better politicians. So I have to ask the church, does this really seem like Christianity to you? We need big governments which aim to help enable us all to most reasonably and efficiently eliminate our basic needs by working collectively together through reasonable taxation, and also taxing and regulating the wealthiest Americans, corporations and the big banks again. Also, if the church doesn't want to see that dreaded one world government currency, then we should be supporting the political party who desires much more regulation on the big banks, which in America is most of the Democrats.

Proverbs 10:15 (NASB)
[15] The rich man's wealth is his fortress,
The ruin of the poor is their poverty.

The Question Which I Believe Is Actually Most Related to Bible Politics in America Today

Which politicians are serving the 400 wealthiest and which politicians are serving the 317 million? The needs of a truly biblically correct government will never be possible through politicians who are serving the 400.

If the Politicians are True to Their Party Today it Looks Like This

Republican politicians work for the 400
Libertarians also far most benefit the 400
Democrats still mainly for the 317,000,000

That is my conclusion. But we still also need to watch every Democrat as well because some of course don't always vote true to the Democratic Party. We must get the big money out of politics from campaign donations to corporate lobbyists for things to start getting better. Also, if the politicians were treated more biblically correct I would think that they should lose their elaborate benefits and retirement pensions and instead receive the same Social Security and Medicare as the rest of us. One thing is for sure. Both of those government services would suddenly become strong again if our nation did this.

Congressional Voting Records Are Most Important!

A politician's words mean very little today, but their congressional voting record means everything. We really need to pay attention to how they are voting on bills.

I recommend *TheMiddleClass.org* for info on this. You can also visit me at *BiblePolitics.com* to see the political stories I am following. Remember to think of voting out the politicians who are serving the 400 wealthiest Americans every time you are driving on a road full of cracks and potholes, and every time you see a need in your community.

Thank you very much for reading *Bible Politics* and for caring about our world's future!

Now let's collectively and religiously VOTE OUT THE OPPRESSORS, EVERYWHERE, ALL OF THEM!

ACKNOWLEDGEMENTS

Much prayer and thought went into *Bible Politics* over the course of about 26 months.

I first want to thank my two awesome and very professional friends who did a better job than I could have ever imagined. I consider both of these people to have been a gift from God to me for this project, and much more a gift as the people they are.

My thanks to Nancy Cleary and all of her staff at Wyatt-MacKenzie Publishing for your thoughtfulness, your focused attention to detail and for all of your amazing work.

Thank you to my friend and best transcriber Dan Pavlosky for the thoughtfulness and attention to detail from beginning to the end.

Also my thanks to you both for your much-valued patience. It was truly a pleasure and honor to work with both of you.

And I thank my friends and family for all of your much-needed prayers and support which made the completion of every chapter possible. I am so blessed to have you all in my life.

Jerry and Joleen Ball

Rick Anderson

Karen O'Farrell

Jan Watkins

And thank you to my late great dad and my sister for helping me decide to write *Bible Politics*.

Joseph M. Bracht

Debbie Lovelace

CPSIA information can be obtained at www.ICGtesting.com
Printed in the USA
BVOW10s0217161013

333880BV00002B/2/P